Learning Library Science Series

Learn

Computer Basics and Its Application in Libraries

Anil K. Dhiman
Yashoda Rani

Ess Ess Publications

4837/24, Ansari Road
Darya Ganj
New Delhi-110 002
Phone: 51563444
Fax: 51563334
E-mail: info@essessreference.com
url: http://www.essessreference.com

First Published 2005

ISBN : 81-7000-457-X

Price : 400/-

Published by :

Ess Ess Publications

4837/24, Ansari Road, Darya Ganj,
New Delhi - 110 002
Phone : 23260807
Fax : 23274173
E-mail: info@essessreference.com
url:http://www.essessreference.com

Printed at :

Printline, New Delhi

Contents

1. **Introduction to Computer** ... 1
Computer : Characteristics, Uses, Types and Functional Parts of Computers; Computer Generation; Computer Languages : Machine Level Language, Assembly Language and High Level Language; Guide Lines for Procuring Hardware.

2. **Role of Computer in Library Automation** ... 41
History of Computers in Libraries; Need of Computerization in Libraries; Computers in CAS/SDI; Library Automation Software Packages: Guidelines to procure them and Discussion on Important Softwares viz.; CDS/ISIS and LIBSYS.

3. **Computerized Service: Library Administrative Service and Information Services** ... 86
Computer Types; Uses of Computer in In-house Automation Activities in Libraries; Planning of Library Automation, MARC Format, CCF and OPACs.

4. **Networking and Networks** ... 110
Communication and Communication Media; Computer Networking: LAN, MAN & WAN; Networking Topologies; Important Networks like CALIBNET, DELNET, INFLIBNET & MALIBNET etc.

5. **Miscellaneous** ... 143
Internet & Its Impact on Library Services; Flow-charting; Softwares; Operating Systems; Bar-coding; E-mail; Number System; Online and Offline Processing; Search Engines; Telecommunication and World Wide Web (www).

Learning Library Science Series

Each book in this series has been written to provide in-depth knowledge of the basics of Library and Information Science and is in accordance with the B.Lib.Sc. syllabus of major Indian universities imparting the said course. To make this work series more comprehensible for the students, the books under this series have been written in Question-Answer format and the language used is very simple, easy and understandable. This series has been divided into six parts, each of which is dedicated to one basic aspect of library and information science.

The present series consists of six books in all, its first part deals with Learn Library and Society, second is Learn Library Management, third is Learn Library Classification (Theory), fourth being Learn Library Classification (Theory), fifth, Learn Reference Services, Information Services and Their Sources and the last and sixth book is Learn Computer Basics and its Application in Libraries. This gives a comprehensive and complete coverage to almost all the syllabi of most of the Indian universities imparting Bachelors' Degree in Library and Information Science (B.Lib.Sc.).

Although this book has primarily been written, keeping in mind the students making an attempt at the above mentioned Degree course, but it is hoped that this book shall find its place with anyone who is interested to know and learn more about the basics of library and information science. Not only the students, but the teachers of library and information science can derive equal benefit from this series. The books are equally suited to librarianship, library science students and library staff seeking to upgrade their skills.

Authors

Acknowledgements

It is indeed difficult to write one book and writing such a series of books is naturally much more difficult but this series could finally see the light of the day, but this could never have been possible without those innumerous books which have been consulted at every step and we are grateful to the authors of all those books, naming all of whom would not be humanly possible. We are thankful to Mrs. Sheel Sethi and Mr. Sumit Sethi, the owners of Ess Ess Publications for giving us an opportunity to present this voluminous work to the readers. We would also like to record our thanks to our friend, Mr. Sushil Kumar of IIT, Roorkee for his kind help. We feel indebted to Sh. Ram Lal Dhiman, Smt. Kamla Devi and Ms. Alka Rani who helped us at various steps. Last but not the least, we are thankful to our son Aman who could not get much of our attention while we were working on this work.

Anil. K. Dhiman
Yashoda Rani

1
Introduction to Computer

Q. : What is computer? Giving various characteristic features of computer, discuss different uses of computers.

Ans. 'Computer' word is derived from Latin word "Computer" which means counting of numbers, counting and accounting machine. Though, the invention of computer was searched basically for mathematical works like additions, deductions, multiplications, divisions with more speedier but today the computer use is mach for non-numerical purposes instead of mathematical purpose. Computers are variously defined by different experts as follows:

- "Computer is an electronic machine, which follows the instructions given and data, which are authentically fed, are accepted and collected and after analyzing data are converted into information which is stored, and retrieval for use."
- "Computer is an electronic machine for general use. It is automated functioning machine based on automation and capable to do all the programmes directed."
- According to *Penguin Dictionary of Computer,* It is "any machine which can accept data in a prescribed form, process the data and supply the result of the processing in a specified format."
- According to *Harrod's Librarians Glossary*, it is "an electronic machine which can accept data, store it, manipulate it as instructed in a programme, retrieve it and convey the result to a user."

Analysing above definitions, it can be said that Computer is an electronic machine, with some mechanical facilities and is mainly used for Data Processing. It performs the arithmetical and logical operations on the input data and gives the desired output. But in between the input and output, is something called processing, which is done by the computer and processing method or steps are provided by the users in terms of logical instruction known as program. Input data are fed into the computer through input device (keyboard etc.) and output is received through output device (Printer, Screen, etc.). It processes no intelligence of its own and it's I.Q. is zero.

Characteristic Features of Computer

The major characteristic features of the computer that make it such powerful machine, are:

1. Speed : Computer works very speedier than human being. It runs and give results with effect of electronic waves. Even general computer of today works in naino seconds and in one second it completes two lacs directions. Thus, there is no any alter of computer. Where high speed calculation is needed, computer is used for related works.

2. Accuracy : The results of computer are always fully correct. Computer once given correct data with correct instructions, it gives correct result. The mistakes seen in results are not created by computer but it is always human error. Sometimes there may be virus attack or mechanical disorder in computer, as a result the mistake is occurred.

3. Storage Capacity: Computer is provided devices for memory, like external and internal collection as a sources by hard disc. Floppy disc, CD-ROM, and thus computer can store data and informations which can be retrieved on need.

4. Capabilities: Computer can do such works which is impossible by human being such as, to make repairing of racket in space having after come out is not difficult. Thus, computer can do most difficult tasks even.

5. Diligence : Computer is an electronic machine, which can work continuously for many hours with the full capacity and thus it never tires or takes rest. If computer is given or fed millions of data it gives uniform results.

6. Versatility : It transfer data to main memory and basic arithmetic and logical operations, along with other operations.

7. Small Size : Computer can collect lot of memories in different data in its internal and external devices. Information world is like ocean in size but it can be stored in a small computer. A small sized floppy can restore more than 100 pages matter and in the same way all the volumes of Encyclopedia Britannica can be stored in the size of 12cm of CD-ROM. Therefore, the informations which is seldom used or to be stored only for future use, can be stored in CD-ROM or in other form, and much space can be saved.

8. Information Retrieval : To get desired information from collection for retrieval, which is very complicate if collection is too large, a computer may analyse the problem and provides the desired information immediately.

9. Automation : Computer saves labour and time both due to its automation system. Computer works continuously for many hours, having after given instructions in proper system.

Uses of Computers

Computers are penetrating in almost every aspect of our lives, to help us to solve problems and arrive at solutions very, quickly and easily. The thinking computer, or what is referred to as artificial intelligence, has been researched upon with favourable results at each stage, and now it has become a reality with wide application. The use of computer in many fields, are as follows:-

1. Scientific Research : Due to invention of computer, the calculations which were out of approach to human, has now become very easy. Many fields of science like physical science, chemical science and chemistry, astrology are developed due to invention of computers. Medicine, research labs, educational institutions are some fields which are given assistance as boon by computer.

2. Business Uses: Computer is used for day work to day and accounting work at large scale within an easy way. Small or large all types of works are being done in industry by the computer making salary bills, sales, insurance, share etc. Even in banks, it serves all the accounting and even withdrawals and deposits through its counters in automated ways.

3. Industrial Use : In large industries, it keeps and maintains accounts, cash book, production plan, cost accounting and cost control and stock control etc.

4. Environmental Uses : Correct forecasting of meteorology is possible with the help of computer. These forecasting by computer gives accurate results and thus can be avoided by loss.

5. Space Technology : First step of the man on the moon was due to Computer. Incidents occurred in the space, can be seen with the help of computer, like location of the planets, its circulation speed etc.

6. Communication : Computer has made the communication system easy. Air wing, control of air travels, training of Pilots, reservation of sheets, preparing of time table, carriage and stock control, goods carrying through rail and roads are the jobs which can be done easily, efficiently and in less time.

7. Educational Field : Computer plays an important role in the field of education. Orders and instructions, lectures and symposiums can be stored for future retrieval and thus it helps in teaching.

8. Use for Libraries : Computer can keep the record of circulation of books to the staff and students and technical works like acquisition of books, classification and cataloguing.

Moreover with the advent of www and Internet, it become very easy to get the information very quickly from the remote places with in a fraction of minutes

Q. : What do you mean by computer? Discuss its functional parts with the help of block diagram.

Or

What do you mean by computer? Discuss various types of computers available today.

Or

Write short notes on the following:

- **Hardware**
- **Block Diagram**
- **ROM**
- **RAM**
- **Input/Output Devices**
- **Mini/Micro Computers**

Ans. Historically speaking, the word computer has been derived from the Latin word *computer* which means to calculate. Therefore, the term 'computer' can logically be applied to any calculating device. However, in common usage, the term has come to refer rather specifically to an electronic computer. Early writers in computer field frequently referred to the equipment as an automatic computer to differentiate it from other calculating devices. As generally understood, Computer is an electronic machine, which is used for performing arithmetic and logical operations, mainly data processing.

Types of Computer

On the basis of operation and power capacity, the computers can be divided in following manner :

(A) On thc basis of operating system

(i) **Analog Computers:** These are the computers that operate on data in the form of continuously variable physical quantities. Data which are obtained through measurement is called continuous data e.g. speedometer thermometer, etc. These computer does specific jobs related with science but these are not useful for libraries.

(ii) **Digital Computer :** These computers manipulate discrete data and performs arithmetic calculations. All computers used for business and scientific applications are digital computers. This type of computers are used in general purposes of library works like arrangement of author list in alphabetical order, to search the isolated words or indexing.

(iii) **Hybrid Computer :** These are the data processing devices using desirable features of both analog and digital machines. They can perform functions like collection of information, its storage, resources, analytical study and representation of the data. For e.g., in a hospital intensive care unit, analog devices may measure a patients body function. These signs may then be converted into numbers and supplied to a digital component in the system.

(B) On the basis of power capacity

(i) **Super Computer :** Super computers are large in size and most powerful computers. Unlimited data can be stored in its internal memory. Its speed and capacity is limited.

They are mainly used in scientific areas of weather forecasting, nuclear weapon development and energy supply and conservation. They are required by large corporations and government agencies, where the need for large databases and complex calculation capabilities may justify the enormous costs involved in their acquisition and maintenance. Crayer of America and NEC of Japan are the example of super computer.

(ii) **Mainframe Computer :** Before the development of the computer of IVth generation the word 'mainframe' was used for these computers to denote central unit. Large and powerful computers were regarded mainframe computer. Earlier micro-computer were not being used as multi-user but mainframe computer were capable to run multi-user projector and analysis of data to speed up.

(iii) **Mini Computers :** The distinction between the mini-computers and the mainframes has become somewhat, blurred. When first introduced, the mini systems had the same types of capabilities as mainframes but contained smaller primary memories and were less powerful than mainframe computers. Cost wise, they were less expensive than the mainframes.

(iv) **Microcomputers :** Microcomputers systems have received a great deal of attention in recent years. These are the smallest, cheapest and commonly used computer systems. These computers were developed in 70's decade. These were called as 'Computer on a Chip' too. On the basis of capacity it can be divided into following types :

   (i) **P.C. :** Micro computer was named as P.C. Its memory and internal storing capacity was low and was useful for very small purposes.

   (ii) **P.C. XT :** It is the detailed form of P.C. and the meaning of XT is the short name of extended technology.

   (iii) **P.C. AT :** It is the revised and refined form of computer and AT is the short form of (Advanced Technology) and its capacity of internal memory is high.

   (iv) **P.C.A.T 386 & 486 :** These are useful machines. For the use of dense and depth, the use of UNIX and DONIX operating systems are used.

   (v) **Pentium :** It is a micro computer on the basis of Pentium 586 chip. Its name is changed into Pentium from PC 586. Now-a-days, Pentium-IV with highest speeds are available in the market.

Computer System Organization

A computer is a fast and accurate system that is organized to accept, store and process the data and produce output results under the direction of a stored programme or instructions. The term "system" is often used in many different ways. But for our purpose a system is a group of integrated parts that have the common purpose of achieving some objectives.

The basic organisation of a computer system consists of following three things:

1. Hardware
2. Software
3. Firmware

(1) HARDWARE

Hardware is a set of physical components which function on applying appropriate, predefined standardized instructions. In other words, we can say that Hardware is the Electronic and Mechanical parts of computer.

The first impression of a computer such as the one shown in the figure is likely to be given by its hardware. The computer itself is surrounded by a set of devices collectively referred to as peripheral equipment, often shortened to peripherals. This term includes the input/output devices such as keyboards, printers, etc. It also includes external memory (also known as secondary memory or backup store) for the long term storage of data.

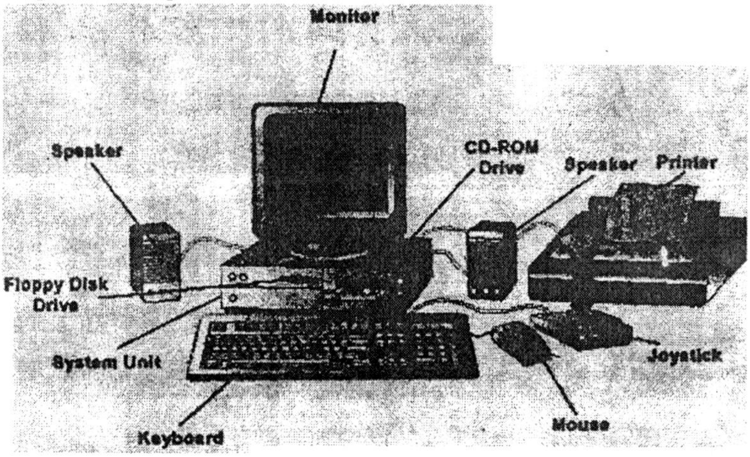

Computer – Hardware

Functional Parts : A 'Computer system' consists of three main functional components or sub-systems: the central processing unit (CPU); the input/output, and the internal memory. These are indicated with the help of a block diagram shown below.

(i) Input Devices : These are the devices responsible for feeding instructions and data. Input devices facilitate the users to translate their data into binary-coded electronic pulses and send them to the computer processor (CPU). Input devices can be connected, disconnected, and reconnected to the computer as and when required. These devices are, therefore, known as peripherals. There are a variety of input devices like keyboard, mouse, card reader, tape drive and disc drive, OCR (optical Character Reader) etc. Keyboard and the mouse are the most widely used input devices.

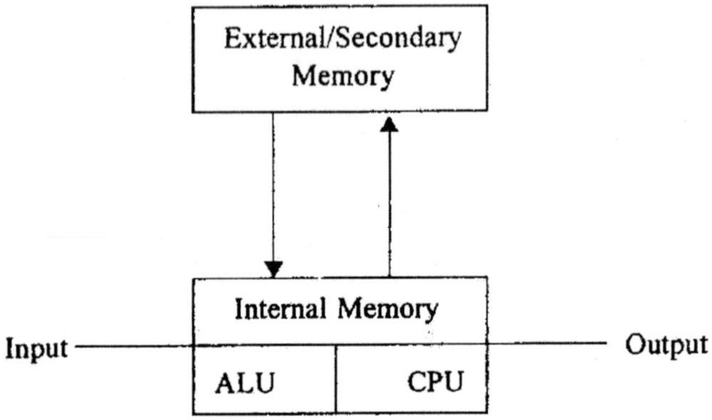

Block Diagram of a computer

(ii) Central Processing Unit (CPU) : The CPU is generally referred to as the brain of the computer system. It is composed of three units: (i) control unit (ii) the arithmetic/logic unit (ALU) and (iii) the primary storage unit. Each of these units performs its unique functions.

(i) **A.L.U.** – It is part of a computer system containing the circuitry that does the addition, subtraction, multiplication, division and comparison.

(ii) **Control Unit** – It is the section of CPU that selects, interprets and controls the execution of the program instructions. Although it does not perform any actual processing on the data, this unit acts as a central nervous system for the other parts of the computer.

There are special memory units inside the CPU, known as Registers, which help in speeding up the rate of data transfer within the CPU. Each register can receive data, store temporarily and pass it to on as and when directed by the control unit. A CPU can have a number of registers and the number of registers varies from computer to computer.

There are some registers which are common to all the computers. These are the Memory Address Register (MAR), Memory Buffer Register (MBR), Program Counter (PC), AC Computer (ACC) and the Instruction Register. The function of these registers are as follows-

MAR – It holds the address of the active memory location.

MBR – It holds the contents of the word read.

PC – It holds the address of the instruction to be executed next.

ACC – The initial data, intermediate results and the final results of processing are kept in this register.

AR – It holds the instruction that is currently being executed

(iii) Memory : It is a device or medium that can accept data, hold them and deliver them on demand at a later time. Primary Memory is mainly to two-types viz. RAM and ROM.

(a) **Random Access Memory (RAM) :** During the execution of a program the data required by program is stored in RAM. It provides a volatile storage i.e., the data are lost in the event of power failure.

(b) **Read Only Memory (ROM) :** The programs, which are always required for running the machine, are stored in ROM. It provides a non-volatile storage, i.e., the data does not get erased even when the power is switched off.

However, the contents of ROM can't be changed but for more specialized uses, where the user may like his own special functions or programs to be performed, it is preferable to use fabricate ROM on which a user can write his own programme. All data are processed in the main memory of the computer while it is permanently stored in secondary memories like floppies, magnetic tapes, hard discs, etc.

(3) Output Devices : Output devices are to collect the results. The popular and widely used output devices are : printers, which provide results on the paper, visual display units (VDUs), which project results on the screen, and magnetic tape and disc drives, which produce machine-readable information on the magnetic media.

(4) External Memory : This is also called auxiliary memory. It provides a non-volatile and less expensive extension to the computers' internal memory. This type of memory is used when internal memory of the computer (RAM) is not sufficient enough to handle large volumes of data or particularly long series of instructions. A number of input/ output devices are used for purpose like Floppy disk, Hard disk, Magnetic disk or tape, CD-ROM and DVD etc.

(II) Software

Software is the means by which the general-purpose hardware of a computer system is made to perform specific tasks. It is nothing but a set of program which has the objectives to enhance the capability of hardware machine.

According to use of software, they can be divided into following categories:

1. Application software
2. System software
3. Custom software

(1) Application Software : It is a set of programs designed to carry out operations for a specified application such as word processing, payroll package, inventory system etc. A word processing software provides facility to enhance the text and modified it. A pay roll package produces pay slips and take care of everything regarding to the pay roll management.

(2) System Software : It is a set of one or more programs to control the application and activity of computer. These software are not for a specific application. These are general software produced to enhance the capabilities of computer and for providing a medium to user to interact with control signals generated by control unit and controlled by application software. Operating system is also a system software. Thus, in order for a computer to produce useful output, the hardware and software must work together. Thus there is a special relationship between hardware and software; both are complementary to each other. Nothing useful can be done with the computer hardware on its own and software can not be utilized without supporting hardware.

Compiler, interpreter, and operating systems are the examples of system software. A compiler translates whole of the high level language source program into a machine code object program prior to the object program being loaded into main memory and executed. Contrast this with the interpreter which deals with the source program one instruction at a time, completely translating and executing each instruction before it goes into the next.

An operating system is a program, which acts as an interface between the computer hardware and the actual user and controls the execution of all type of programs. It is an integrated set of programs that is used to manage the various resources and overall operations of a computer system. It not only supports the activities of a computer installation but also its prime objective is to improve the performance and efficiency of a computer system and increase facility, the ease with which a system can be used. Thus, like a manager of a company, an operating system is responsible for the smooth and efficient operation of the computer system. MS-DOS, Microsoft Windows, IBM OS/2 are examples of operating systems.

Depending upon the number of users, the operating system may be:

(i) **Single User Operating systems :** In this case, CPU performs only one job at a time i.e., at any instant only one user can work on the machine and only one program can be loaded in the memory for execution. These systems have a single processor. MS-DOS is the most common example of such an operating system.

(ii) **Multi-User Operating system -** In this case, multiple users can work on the computer, each performing different tasks. More than one program will reside in the memory as there are many users connected to the same computer and waiting for the processor to finish the execution of the program. Examples of multi-user operating systems are Windows NT, UNIX.

The role of the operating system is to complement the hardware by providing a layer of services which manage the resources of the hardware and permit the users to drive the system. In brief, an operating system performs the following functions:

(i) **Processor management :** assignment of processors to different tasks being performed by the computer system.

(ii) **Memory management :** allocation of main memory and other storage areas to the system programs as well as user programs and data.

(iii) **Input/Output management :** co-ordination and assignment of the different input and output devices while one or more programs are being executed.

(iv) **File management :** storage of files on various storage devices and the transfer of these files from one storage device to another. It also allows all the files to be easily changed and modified through the use of text editors or some other file manipulation routines.

(v) **Command Interpreter:** Interpretation of commands and instructions.

(3) Custom Software : These software relates with a specific project and the help of another software. These softwares are made for a specific purposes by specific persons.

(III) Firmware

Firmware is often used to provide very basic services at a functional level just above the hardware (e.g. the bios in PC). The boundary between hardware and firmware is imprecise and in any case, is not important for most users.

Actually these are the ROMs, the second type of memory used in personal computes, in addition to read only memory (RAM). As the ROM chips have software programs permanently etched into their circuitry, these are often referred to as Firmware – because it's kind of halfway between hardware and the software. For example, it ensures that if you press 'one' on the keyboard, the digit 1 appears on the screen. It also handles the basic needs of the hardware involved, which include all I/O devices.

Q. : Write a short-note on Input/Output devices.

Ans. Input or output devices are the means which establish the communication between the system and its user. Input devices are used to get information into the CPU and memory of the system while an output device is used to retrieve the information from the system. Most of the devices which are being used as input device, may be used as an output device or vice versa, e.g. Floppy disk, Magnetic disk, Magnetic tape etc. But some exceptions are there e.g. Printer, which is used only as an output device and a keyboard is used only as an input device. Some of the important I/O devices are –

(i) **Punched Card:** Early to inventions of keyboard, floppy disc, etc. punch cards were being used for data entry. There were different punch for different words representing, for data entries. But they were perishable and capacity to data entry was very meager.

(ii) **Keyboard :** Keyboard is the most important and useful device. It is always used to provide data to the computer therefore it is adjacent part of the computer. It is like typewriter machine and likewise typewriter, the data are entered by typing with the help of keyboard.

(iii) **Mouse:** The Mouse is a palm-size device with a ball built into the bottom. It is usually connected to the computer by a cable and may have from one to four button (usually two) and comes in many shapes and sizes. When the mouse is moved over a smooth surface, the balls rolls, and the pointer on the display screen moves in the same direction. With the mouse, one can draw, select options from a menu and modify or move the text. In addition to minimizing typing errors, a mouse makes operating a microcomputer easier for beginning users.

(iv) **Hard Disk :** A hard disk is a disk made of metal and covered with magnetic recording surface. It holds data represented by presence (1) and absence (0) of magnetized spots. Hard disk drives read and write data in much the same way that diskette drives do, however it significantly differs in three ways. Hard disk devices can handle thousand times more data than diskettes. Hard disk drives are usually built into the system cabinet and not removable. Hard disks a read and write data faster than diskettes.

(v) **Floppy disk :** The floppy disk gets its name from the fact that it is made of flexible plastic material. This plastic base is coated with an iron oxide, recording substance that is similar to the material applied to the plastic ribbon of a magnetic tape. Data are recorded as tiny visible magnetic spots on this coating.

(vi) **Magnetic disk :** Magnetic disk is round platters coated with magnetic recording material. They come in different size. Data are stored on all disks in a number of invisible concentric circles called tracks.

(vii) **CD-ROM :** It's size is 12 cm and its full name is 'compact disc read only memory' and maximum data than floppy can be collected in it. Its information can be read only and no addition and alteration is possible. In order to use CD-ROM, there should be a drive for the operation of CD-ROM in the computer, thus it can be used as a device. CD-ROM can hold graphics, text, sound and full motion video. A single CD-ROM can contain up to 650 to 700 MB of data, enough to comfortably house an entire encyclopaedia. Now-a-days, re-writable CDs are also coming.

(viii) **Visual Display Unit :** A device capable of displaying keyed input and CPU output on a Cathode Ray Tube. It looks like a television and is used to display the input data, messages and processed information from the computer.

(ix) **Scanner :** The scanners are also used as input device. There are a number of situations when some information (picture or text) is available on paper and is needed on the computer disk for further manipulation. The simplest way would be to take a photograph of the image directly from the source and convert it into a form that can be saved on the disk. A scanner scans an image and transforms the image to ASCII codes (the code used by a computer to represent the characters you find on your keyboard-letters of the alphabet, numbers, punctuation, marks, etc.) and graphics. These can be edited, manipulated and combined and then printed.

Scanners are of two types – the flatbed type and the roller-feed type. While in a roller-feed scanner, the image is passed over a roller where it is captured whereas the flat bed variety works like a photocopier. Flat bed scanners can scan and store images from books without having to remove the page, which is difficult in the case of the roller feed variety.

Many of the scanners available nowadays, are capable of not only scanning text and graphics but also integrating text and graphics files. Scanners are used to reproduce photographs on the computer screen. They can be employed in training programmes and in desktop publishing. In business, scanners may also be used for storing documents on the computer.

(x) **Printer :** The available desired information from the computer can be seen on screen like T.V and if needed it can be given command for printing too and it is being done with the help of Printer, a device. At present there are so many printers available in the market. Some of them are as follows:-

(a) **Dotmatrics Printer :** The words or numbers to be printed by this printer is being written in dot or points (.) therefore, it is named as Dotmatrics. It can print 30 to 300 words or figures in a second.

(b) **Line Printer :** It's speed is more than Dotmatrics and it prints one line in a turn.

(c) **Laser Printer :** It is based on electro-photography. It's speed is very high and sound less while printing. It prints one page at a time.

Q. : Write an essay on different generations of computers.

Or

What is computer? Write an essay on evolution of computers.

Or

What do you understand by 'Computer Generation'? Explain some of the distinguishing features of 4th and 5th generation of computers.

Or

Write short notes on 4th and 5th Generation of Computers.

Ans. Computer has an important and specific place in the inventions invented in human civilization so far. It is one of the strange inventions which gave a new rise and shape to the history and development of culture and civilization. The invention of modern computer was invented and started with the day and moment when human felt a need of more easy, speedy and efficient method of counting and calculation instead of finger printing as its replaced device. Such first attempt was the formation of Abacus. It was a clay board with number of grooves in which pebbles were placed. These pebbles were moved from one side to another for counting. Later as early as 1600, machines to perform arithmetic operations were developed by Pascal and Leibnitz and such efforts continued over the years, each effort leading to the betterment and perfection of the calculating machines.

The first machine employing concepts similar to those of a computer was the *analytical engine* designed by Charles Babbage, a

British Mathematician in 1833. The analytical engine contained many features similar to those found in today's computers. It incorporated a punch card input, a memory unit or store, an arithmetic unit, an output unit and a control with accuracy upto twenty places.

Since the, number of changes were made and various machines made from time to time. The first real step towards the development of computer as we know it, was made in the year 1944 by Howard Aiken of Harvard University. He developed the first automatic calculator, which was called *Mark-1.* It was an electronic computer, but utilized electromagnetic relays and mechanical counters. Instructions were fed to Mark-1 by means of holes in a punched paper tape and the result was obtained in the form of holes punched in cards. Mark-1 was electromechanical rather than an electronic device. The first electronic computer, i.e., the Atanasoff Berry Computer, was designed in 1942 by John Vincent Atanasoff and Clifford Berry.

The evolution of modern computer can be viewed in specific generations. Over the period from the early 1940s to the present, computer scientists have been able to identify clear-cut stages in the development of computer technology and systems. With each stage radical breakthroughs in electronics have occurred, with the result that the computers based upon the older technology of electronics have been replaced by a *newer form of machines.* These have been named *'generations'* where each computer generation had certain unique characteristics or properties. Four generations of computers have been identified so far and the race is on for the fifth generation.

First Generation

Until 1951, electronics computers were the exclusive possession of scientists and the military. Till then, nobody tried to use them for business purpose. The idea of marketing them was conceived by Mauchly and Eckert, creators of ENIAC's. As US census bureau was already using IBCP cards, they were the pioneers in buying this computer for the first time in 1951. The company created by Mauchley and Eckert, became UNIVAC division of Sperry and Corporation (later known as UNISYS).

The bringing of first UNIVAC general purpose electric digital computer, marks the beginning of the first generation of electronic computers.

These computers used valves and all the components were joined by copper wires. Due to large size of the components and due to the facts that the components had to be spaced apart as the valves dissipated a lot of heat, the computers were very bulky and required huge electric power, airconditioners, maintenance and space for their installation. Further, the speed of operation was very slow and had a very low reliability factor as vacuum tubes failed frequently. They were still given the name of "electronic brains" by the journalist. They also said that these electronic brains will change the world one-day. Later IBM corporation developed IBM 701, IBM 702 and IBM 650 and few other systems. These were called the first generation computers. The popular brand of first generation computer was IBM 650, which had a magnetic drum memory and utilized punch cards for input and output. This type of computer was of an intermediate size and was designed to meet the requirements of business and scientific applications. The available memories ranged from a few hundred thousand words of main storage. The cycle time was of the order of few milliseconds. It was only after 1957 that magnetic tapes were introduced as a faster and convenient storage medium. A single tape could hold approximately 1100 P cards (i.e., about 2 pages of information).

IBM made 19 IBM 701 computers and at that time industry felt that these computers are sufficient enough to take care of American business. These computer required special facilities and highly trained personnel. The instructions given to these computers, were in machine language (i.e. 0's and 1's). As the language was tough and understood by very few people. There were very few personnel available for it.

Computer belonging to this generation had the following characteristics:

(i) Comparatively large in size as compared to present day computers.

(ii) Generated lot of heat, they were not consistent and reliable as the valves tended to fail frequently.

(iii) Low capacity internal storage.

(iv) Individual, non-related models.

(v) Processors operated in the milliseconds speed range.

(vi) Internal storage consisted of magnetic drum and delay lines.

Second Generation

First Generation Computers were very unreliable, mainly because of vacuum tubes which kept on burning out. Users had to be prepared all the time with dozen of extra tubes to replace them. The computers of second generation were characterized by the use of Solid State Devices (transistors) instead of vacuum-tubes. Transistorized circuits were smaller and generated little heat, were less expensive and consumed less power than vacuum tube circuits and were much greater in processing capacity. Since transistors had a faster switching action, this generation computers were significantly faster and smaller and were more reliable too than first generation computers. The use of magnetic cores as the primary internal storage medium and the introduction of removable magnetic disc pack were other major developments of the second generation. Although magnetic tapes were still used commonly. These computers had built in error detecting devices and more efficient means were developed to input and retrieve from the computer. They were easier to work with. More efficient programming methods and higher level languages like FORTRAN and COBOL became available. These were easily understandable by people especially because no codes like assembly language had to be remembered by the programers. Moreover, unlike assembly language the high level language were not machine specific i.e. same set of programs could be used on computers produced by different manufactures. The instruction cycle time dropped from several hundred microseconds of the first generation in tens of micro- seconds of the second generation. The main memory in these systems could store several hundred thousand words.

This generation of computers could communicate with others using telephone lines. Transmission of data from one computer to another was also possible in this generation. Although, the processing was very slow but the idea was convenient which was further developed in next generations. The problems which second-generation computer faced was that input and output devices were too slow. The projects started in second generation to solve these problems. They used second generation technology but finally proposed results in third generation.

Dr Daniel Slotnick worked out first solution, when he was working with Burroughs Corporation, at that time. He designed a computer for US department of Defence and tried to solve the problem of machines sitting idle waiting for input and output. The computer known as ILLIAC IV was developed. It was having 4 control units and thus was able to perform input/output and processing (mathematical operation) at the same time. Slotnick was granted a patent for "Parallel Processing". They were also called as first super computer. The second super computer was proposed by MIT (Massachusetts Institute of Technology) by a group of students and professors. The name of the project was MAC (Multiple Access Computer) and concept of multiprogramming was developed there. The system could process the programs concurrently which were run by different users.

Some of the popular models in this generation of computer systems, include IBM-1401, IBM-1620, BURROUGHS B-200 SERIES, HONEY-WELL H-400, NATIONAL CASH REGISTER NCR-315, 500 and UNIVAC-1004. Many of these computers were used for business applications.

Computers of this generation had the following characteristics:

(i) Smaller in size as compared to the first generation computers.

(ii) Generated a lower level of heat, as components were much smaller.

(iii) Greater degree of reliability because of solid state technology.

(iv) Higher capacity of internal storage.

(v) Use of core storage instead of magnetic drum and delay lines.

(vi) Related series of processors - the family concept.

(vii) Processor operated in the microsecond speed.

(viii) High cost direct accesses storage.

Third Generation

A revolution in the computer developments took place with the development of integrated circuits (IC) on a single silicon chip. In 1958, Jack St Clair Kelby and Robert Noyce invented the first IC. IC incorporated number of transistors and electronic circuits on a single wafer or chip of silicon. This ushered in the third generation of computer systems in 1964. The integrated circuits enhanced considerably the processing capability and the speed of the computer. During the period 1964 to 1970, capability of placing 12 or more logic gates on a single chip was developed into a well-defined technology of small- scale integration (SSI). A logic gate is a circuit to perform arithmetic of addition, subtraction, multiplication or division. In 1970, this technology was redefined to a point where hundreds or more gates could be placed on a chip of silicon and incorporated as functional logic block in an overall system. This technology was termed as middle scale integration (MSI). There was intense pressure on the semiconductor manufacturers to provide greater densities of gates on a single integrated circuit chip. Consequently, more complex chips were developed with the ultimate goal of obtaining a central processor on a single physical circuits element. These circuits had higher reliability and lower power consumption and substantially reduced size. Component densities of 1,000 to 10,000 gates on a single silicon chip became possible. The technology consisting of 1,000 gates per chip, termed large-scale integration (LSI), started to become commercially viable in 1975. The later technology consisting of more than 10,000 gates per chip is called very large scale integration (VLSI) or grand scale integration (GSI). These circuit become very useful in assembling computers. Some of the popular third generation computers are-IBM-360, series, IBM-370 series and ICL-2900 series. The large-advanced computer systems are usually called 'Main Frame'.

Integrated circuits technology is responsible for bringing in revolution in the computer industries. Scientists were aware that more powerful computers can be built by building more complex circuits, but as these circuits had to be wired by hand, these computer were too complex and expensive. IC solved this problem by introducing a computer that costed lower then first generation computer and offered more memory and faster processing. In 1962, a new company built a plant in "Silicon Valley", near Sanjose, California. DEC (Digital Equipment Corporation) revolutionised the total computer industry with this computer which used IC's.

The first commercially available minicomputer was introduced in 1965. The PDB-8 (Programmed Data Processor) could fit easily in the corner of a room and did not require any attendant to it. The computer could be accessed by number of users from different locations of the building. That was actually implementing time-sharing, which was developed in second generation. The price was one tenth of the traditional main frame, which made it possible for smaller companies to afford.

IBM was dominant in the market by releasing 360 series of computer. They were of different sizes of main frame computers. The main advantage of using this computer was use of same machine language compatibility thus making it easy and cost effective specially when upgraded. By 1967, IBM decided to change its track as number of programming language came in the market. This was the beginning of software industry as the languages grew and people who had the skills to translate user requirements in these languages were high on demand now.

Dr. Hopper told about the origin of Bug and Debug in her book "Understanding Computers". It was 1965, when students were working on Mark II and it stopped working. Programmers kept trying to figure out what's wrong with the computer, finally discovered that there was a moth caught in one of the relays causing the whole trouble. They removed it and the computer started working fine. Hence, the terms "Bug" and "Debug" were introduced. The first bug can still be seen taped on a page in a logbook at the Naval Weapons Museum in Dahlgren, Virginia.

Computers of this generation have the following characteristics:

1. Smaller in size as compared to second generation computers.
2. Higher capacity internal storage.
3. Remote communication facilities.
4. Multiprogramming facilities.
5. Reduced cost of direct access storage.
6. Processors, which operate in nanosecond speed range.
7. Ranges of computers with a common architecture whereby models were upward compatible.
8. Use of high level languages such as COBOL.
9. Wide range of optional peripherals.

Fourth generations

The 1970's marked the beginning of a new generation of computers, produced by computer giants like IBM, ICL, NCR and Burrought. From design viewpoint, the new generation provided increased input-output capability, longer component life as well as greater system reliability. From the functional view point, new powerful language were developed to broaden the use of multiprogramming and multiprocessing and major shift from batch processing to on line, remote interactive processing.

The development of microprocessor chip, which contains an

entire central processing unit (CPU) on a single silicon chip led to the mushroom growth of inexpensive computers. They were not computers by themselves but they could perform all the functions of arithmetic logic unit and control units of the CPU. When these microprocessors were connected with memory and input-output devices, they became microcomputers. The semiconductor memories were also very small and very cheap. There were several types of memory chips. Three of the most commonly used are - (a) Random Access Memory (RAM) in which data can be read or written corresponding to the main memory of the conventional computer, (b) Read Only Memory (ROM) and (c) Programmable Read Only Memory (PROM).

The fourth generation of computers may be called microcomputer generation. The input-output devices used with the fourth generation computers were quite advanced. Among the advanced input-output devices employed in fourth generation computers are optical, readers by which whole documents can be fed into the computer, audio response terminals by which an operator can vocally introduce data or instructions and graphic display terminals by which an operator can feed pictures into the computer.

The use of very large integrated circuits (VLSI) has made the fourth generation computers very compact, much less expensive, faster, more reliable and of much greater data processing capacity than equalized third generation computers.

Some computers belonging lo fourth generation are DEC-10, STAR-1000, PDP-11 and APPLE Series Personal Computers.

Fifth Generation

Till fourth generation of computers, the major stress was on improving the hardware from valves to transistors and then to integrated circuits, which resulted in miniaturization and fast speed of computers. However, the lack of thinking power has forced the scientists to work further for fifth generation computers. The concept of "Artificial Intelligence" is being used in these computers and Japanese call them "Knowledge Processors". Automatic programming, computational logic, pattern recognition and control of robots, the processes which need skill and intelligence are examples of Artificial Intelligence. These computers, when developed, will be able to execute billions of instructions per second and will have unimaginable storage capacities. The present day high level languages will become obsolete on these

Comparison of Different Generations of Computers

First Generation	Second Generation	Third Generation	Fourth Generation	Fifth Generation
Vaccume tubes used in electronic circuits	Use of transistors	Use of integrated circuits	Use of VLSI techniques	These machines will be different from earlier four generations both conceptually and functionally
Had very small internal memories based on relays or magnetic drums	Utilised magnetic core for internal memory	Magnetic core and solid state main storage	Increased storage capacity and speed of operation	The new machines would be known as Knowledge Information Processing Systems (KIPS)
Machines were physically large and utilized punched card for input	Possessed increased storage capacity	More flexibility input/ output which is disk oriented	Modular design and compatibility between equipment (hardware) provided by different manufacturers	They are going to be based on sophisticated electronics and artificial intelligence
Slow input/output devices	Use of high level programming languages such as FORTRAN, COBOL etc.	Smaller in size, better performance and reliability	Availability of sophisticated programs	They will have natural language interface using knowledge processing systems and problem solving software, utilize parallel processing
Low level symbolic	The machines of this	Extensive use of higher	Greater versatility	Characteristics such as voice

First Generation	Second Generation	Third Generation	Fourth Generation	Fifth Generation
languages were used for programming purposes	generation were smaller in size and produced less heat during operation	level programming languages		recognition, speech synthesis and image processing are going to be associated with the machines
Less reliable	Utilized tape oriented faster I/O devices	Remote processing and time sharing through communications	Greater versatility of I/O devices	Presently only laboratory prototypes are stated to be under experimentation
Intense air conditioning was required	Credited with speed of operation and reliability	Availability of operating system	Internal memory based on semiconductor devices	—
Slow in operation (1/1000th second) per instruction	Useful for batch oriented applications	Usability for on-line processing speed of operation in the order of nano second range	Advent of micro-processors and micro computers	—
Example : UNIVAC I. IBM 650.	Example of machines; IBM 1401, Honeywell 200	Example : IBM 360	Example : STAR-1000, APPLE-series, PC	—

machines and new computer languages and related software will be needed.

The fifth generation gives the highest priority to making systems that are easy and natural to use. Its other objective relates to the types of technological support needed to support "problem solving systems" according to the fifth generation committee. "In these systems", the committee adds," Intelligence will be greatly improved to approach that of a human being. When compared to conventional systems, the man-machine interface will be closer to that of human behaviour." The fifth generation has three functional requirements:

— easy to use computers with high intelligence and natural human input and output mechanism;

— reliable and efficient software development by new languages, new computer architectures and systems software which overcome previous problems and

— improved overall functions and performance aimed at making computers smaller, lighter, faster, of greater capacity, more flexible and more reliable.

Q. : Write an essay on Computer Languages.

Or

Write short notes on following:

- **Machine Language**
- **High-level language**
- **Assembly language**

Ans. : To take results from the computer, it has to given command. These commands are given in any of language. The process of giving command to the computer is called programming, and to understand the computer, efforts are made for easy programming languages.There are a variety of different programming languages, each of which has been designed to facilitate the coding of a specific kind to application. There are basically three kinds of programming language.

1. Machine Language
2. Assembly Language
3. High-level Language

1. Machine Language

The entire working process of a computer is being done by digits. These digits relates with electric current. General computer can understand two dimensional digits-(bits) language and it is called machine language. This language is formed with two digits (0) and (1) with different connecting additions and multiplications or divisions and deductions. Computer is unable to understand ordinal natural languages, therefore to understand artificial cardinal language is made by (Bites). But there are some limitations of machine language, which are:

(i) Programs written in machine code are not portable between different machines, and each time a new machine is manufactured or acquired, machine code programs will need to be re-written.

(ii) To program in machine code, a programmer must have an intimate knowledge of the working of that particular computer.

(iii) Programs are generally longer than equivalent programs written in a high-level language.

(iv) Machine code is quick in computer operation and makes economical use of computer time. Thus, parts of programs that are executed frequently are usually written in machine code.

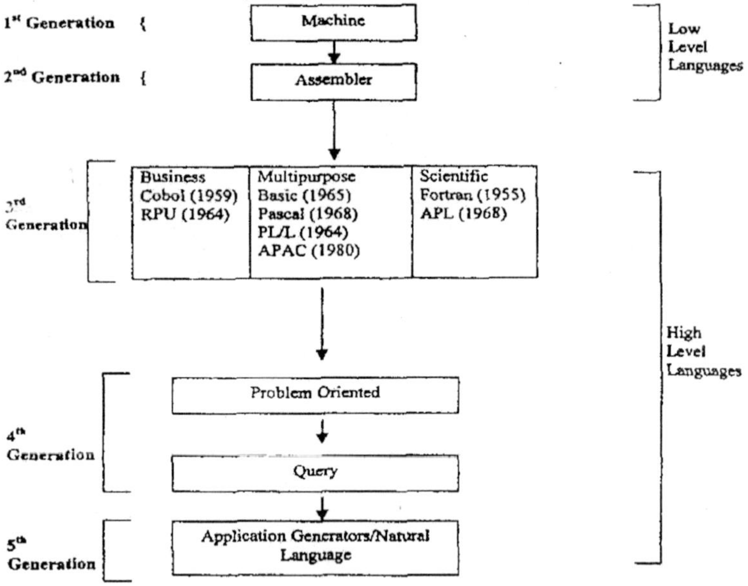

Hierarchy of Programming languages

2. Assembly language

Assembly code language make some concessions to the programmer in that they use mnemonic literal sequences to designate machine codes and to reference storage locations.

Assembly code language do not appear as the '0's and '1's of machine code, and a program in assembly code must be translated into machine code before it can be run. Programs in assembly code language are translated into machine code by a language program known as an Assembler, which acts in a similar way to an automatic bilingual dictionary. Thus,

Program in assembly code	—— Assembler ——→	Program in machine code

Although assembly code is more mnemonic than machine code it is still specific to a group of machines. Some assembly code languages are quite well established, e.g. PLAN for the ICL/900 range, BAL for the IBM360 and 370 series and USERCODE for the ICL System 4 series. This means that:

(i) Programs written in assembly code language are limited in their portability.

(ii) A programmer will need to learn a new language when he transfers between machines.

(iii) Programs in assembly code are still fairly long, not always easy to read and may be prone to mistakes.

(iv) Assembly code is executed quickly and, therefore, is often used for those parts of a set of programs that will be used frequently.

(v) Programs written in assembly code are essentially in the same format as the machine code instruction format. Assembly code language are, for this reason, said to be computer oriented or machine oriented.

But the Assembly languages have the following advantages over machine languages :

(i) Easier to understand and use : Assembly languages are easier to understand and use because mnemonics are used instead of numeric op-codes and suitable names are used for data. The use of mnemonics means that comments are usually not needed; the program itself is understandable. Symbolic programming also saves a lot of time and effort of the programmer because it is easier to write as compared to machine language programs.

(ii) Easy to locate and correct errors : While writing programs in assembly language, fewer errors are made, and those that are made, are easier to find and correct because of the use of mnemonics and symbolic field names. Further more, assemblers are so designed that they automatically catch the errors. If we use an invalid mnemonic or a name that has never been defined, the assembler will print out an error indication. For example, suppose one instruction in the symbolic program reads ADD AREA and we forget to define what AREA is, the assembler will look through its table to find AREA and not finding it will indicate the error.

(iii) Easier to modify : Assembly language programs are easier to modify than machine-language programs. This is mainly because they are easier to understand and hence it is easier to locate, correct and modify instructions as and when desired. Moreover, insertion or removal of certain instructions from the program does not require change in the address part of the instructions following that part of the program, which is required in case of the machine language.

(iv) No worry about addresses : One of the greatest advantage of assembly language is that it eliminates worry about address for instructions and data. This is more important than it seems at first glance. Suppose, we have written a long machine language program involving many steps and many references to itself within the program, such as looping and address modifications and so on. At the very end, we may suddenly discover that we have left out an instruction in the middle. If we insert that instruction, we will have to remember all the following instructions and go through the entire program to check any references to other steps. This is not so in case of assembly languages.

In addition to the above mentioned advantages, an assembly language program also enjoys the efficiency of its corresponding machine code because there is one to one correspondence between the instructions of an assembly language program and its corresponding machine language program. Except for pseudo-instructions, which are simply instructions to the assembler, every other instruction of an assembly language program is translated into one machine language instruction. For every machine language instructions, there is a corresponding symbolic.

3. HIGH-LEVEL LANGUAGE

High level language is like natural language. High-level language enable the construction of program statements having a greater affinity with problem definition; that is they are written in something close to English language. These are known as problem oriented languages. They are not machine dependent. They can incorporate standard processing routines supplied ready-made by the manufacturer. A program in a high level language must be converted into machine code before it can be executed.. This conversion can be performed with the aid of either a compiler or an interpreter. Thus:

Program in high-level language	Compiler or ⟶ Interpreter	Program in machine code

A compiler or an interpreter performs a similar function for high-level languages as does an assembler for Assembly code.

At present there are so many high languages are in use. Each language of these is suitable for a region. The main high languages are as follows:-

(i) **BASIC** : 'Beginners All Purposes Symbolic Instruction Code' was developed by Kerney and Thomas Kurtz at Darth Mouth College in the late 1960s. It was a simple language to be used for teaching programme concepts. However it became very popular and was used for a wide range of business and other applications.

(ii) **COBOL** : It is an abbreviated name of 'Common Business Oriented Language'. COBOL was developed specially for business data processing. It was introduced by the US industry/ government committee in 1960. It is used for large business and commercial applications such as handling of ledgers, accounts, payroll, files etc. It supports simple and limited numeric operations but it can handle complex non numeric operations. It employs commonly used business terms. Its English like statements can be understood very easily, for example

SUBTRACT. WITHDRAWALS FROM OLD BALANCE, GIVING NEW BALANCE.

Its drawback is that it is not a compact language. It is not easy to learn, and it cannot handle complex mathematical computations as FORTRAN does.

(iii) **FORTRAN (Formula Translation) :** Fortran was developed by IBM in 1957 as a language that was convincing used for expressing formulae, writing equations and performing repetitive calculations. FORTRAN was used mainly for scientific applications.

(iv) **PASCAL :** It was developed in 1968 by Nikaus Wirth, who named it after the French Blaise Pascal. Its instructions are made up of algebraic-like expressions and certain English words such as BEGIN, END, READ, WRITE, IF, THEN, REPEAT, WHILE, DO etc. In this respect Pascal resembles many other high-level languages. It also contains some unique features, however, that have been specifically designed to encourage the use of structured programming-an orderly, disciplined approach toward programming that promotes clear, efficient, error-free programs. For this reason, many educators and Professional Programmers favour the uses of Pascal over other general-purpose languages.

Advantages of High Level Languages

High level language enjoy the following advantages over assembly and machine languages:

(i) **Machine independence :** High-level language are machine independent. This is a very valuable advantage because it means that a company changing computers even to one form a different manufacturer - will not be required to rewrite all the programs that are currently using. Even for programs written in the high-level language, some modifications are almost always required, but these modifications are relatively minor and can be easily done without much effort. In other words, a program written in a high-level language can be run on many different types of computers with very little or practically no effort.

(ii) **Easy to learn and use :** These languages are very similar to the language normally used in our day-to-day life, hence they are easy to learn and use. The programmer need not learn anything about the computer he is going to use. He need not worry about how to store his numbers in the computer, where to store them, what to do with them, etc. That is the programmer need not know the machine instructions, the data format and so on. However, such a knowledge is desirable since it allows the programmer to utilize the system more efficiently.

(iii) **Fewer errors :** In case of high level languages, since the programmer need not write all the small steps carried out by the computer, he is much less likely to make an error. The computer takes care of all the little details and will not introduce any error of its own unless something breaks down. Furthermore, compilers are so designed that they automatically catch and point out the errors made by the programmer. Hence, diagnostic errors, if any, can be easily located and corrected by the programmer.

(iv) **Lower program preparation cost :** Writing programs in high-level languages requires less time and effort which ultimately leads to lower program preparation cost. Generally, the cost of all phases of program preparation (coding, debugging and testing etc.) is lower with a high-level language than with an assembly language or with a machine language.

(v) **Better documentation :** A high-level language is designed in such a way that its instructions may be written more like the language of the problem. Thus, the statements of a program written in a high-level language scan be easily understood by a person familiar with the problem. For the documentation of such programs, very few or practically no separate comment and statements are required.

(vi) **Easier to maintain :** Programs written in high level languages are easier to maintain than assembly language or machine language programs. This is mainly because they are easier to understand and hence it is easier to locate, correct and modify the instructions as and when desired. Insertion or removal of certain instructions from a program is also possible without any complication. Thus, major changes can be incorporated with very little effort.

Disadvantage of High-level Languages

Two main disadvantages of high-level languages are:

(i) **Lower efficiency** : Generally a program written in assembly language or machine language is more efficient than one written in high-level languages. That is why the programs written in high-level languages take more time to run and require more main storage.

(ii) **Lack of flexibility** : As the automatic features of high-level languages always occur and are not under the control of the programmer, they are less flexible than assembly languages. An assembly language provides programmers access to all the special features of the machine they are using. Certain types of operations which are easily programmed using the machine's assembly language, are impractical to attempt using a high-level language. This lack of flexibility means that some tasks cannot be done in a high-level language, or can be done only with great difficulty.

Q. : Write an essay on different generations of computer languages.

Or

Write short on :

– 4 GLS Languages

Ans. : The programmer, designer and implementer of a programming language must understand the historical evolution of languages in order to appreciate why different features are present. For instance, younger languages discourage the use of 'Go To' statement as inferior control mechanism and that is correct in the context of current philosophies of software engineering and structured, modular programming.

The overall development of Computer Languages can be better understand through various generations of computer Languages.

1. First-Generation languages

The first generation of computer languages were machine language where instructions were specified in binary notation. It was very difficult to write computer programs using binary notation and it called for intimate knowledge of the machine architecture. In the 1950s assemblers were developed to translate symbolic instruction codes into the ones and zeros of machine instruction codes. A successful high-level language was developed between 1954 and 1958. These-first-generation languages introduce many other basic ideas of high level languages. They are the direct predecessors of the more well known second-generation languages developed between 1957 and 1961. The examples are FORTRAN II, ALGOL60, COBOL and LISP.

2. Second-Generation Languages

ALGOL 60 developed between 1957 and 1960, plays a major role in the development of high-level languages. ALGOL 60 introduces the high level language concepts of nested block structures, scope rule for variables, explicit type declarations for variables and call by value and call by name for passing procedure parameters. It also introduces the 'if-then-else' statement as a selection mechanism, for statement and the while concept for loop control, the local variables and the switch concepts.

ALGOL 60 has three built in data types; integer, real and Boolean.

COBOL was developed between 1959 and 1961 as a business oriented programming language.

LISP was also developed in the period between 1959 and 1961. It is a list processing language that maps programs uniformly on to list structures.

3. Third-Generation Languages

The third generation language came into use in the 1960s and were called high level languages. Example include FORTRAN, COBOL and ALGOL. FORTRAN and ALGOL were designed for scientific computation and COBOL for business applications.

Other third-generation languages developed in the 1960's include the following:

(i) APL, like LISP is an applicative language.

(ii) SNOBOL 4 was developed between 1962 and 1967. SNOBOL-4 is also a dynamically typed language.

(iii) BASIC is another third-generation language. BASIC is simple interactive language that is widely used as a first language for beginning programmers.

(iv) The C language also developed at AT&T Bell Laboratories, which supports and encourages structured programming. It is efficient in its use of primitive machine instructions making it ideal for writing low-level operating system function.

4. Fourth-Generation Languages

Most of the fourth generation developed in the 1970s evolved from PASCAL. These languages were developed keeping in the mind, the following objectives –

- Speed up the development of applications.
- Make changes easy and quick to achieve.
- Minimise debugging efforts.
- Generate, bug-free codes from high level expressions of requirements.
- Be user-friendly.

There is no agreed definition as to what constitutes a Fourth Generation Language. It might be safer to suggest that it consists of everything which is not in the first three categories.The following is a checklist of desirable features for 4GL evaluation and this is summarized below.

* Centered around a relational database.
* Links to other proprietary databases and other non-database files. This will permit gradual transition to the new development strategy.
* Integrated and active data dictionary.
* Simple Query Language may use a syntactical structure.
* Query by forms.
* Integrated Screen Design Tool.
* Dialogue Design Tool including generation and manipulation of business graphics.
* Report generator.
* Procedural Coding facility. This may be done directly through a conventional language (say COBOL) or indirectly viz. a code Design Aid (such as an Action Diagrammer).
* Non-Procedural Programming code.
* Spreadsheets and graphics.

The major fourth-generation languages include, SAS (a statistical analysis languages), FOCUS (a data retrieval language),

RENDEZVOUS (a conversational data retrieval language), PROLOG (an inferential expert system language), as well as CUPID, FLORAL, SQUARE, RAMS, d-BASE IV, FOXPRO-2.6, COLINGO, Sybase, FOCUS, SQL, NOMAD, ORACLE, POWER BUILDER, VISUAL C++, VISUAL BASIC, Java and others.

Table showing Difference between 3 GLS and 4 GLS

Third-generation Languages	Fourth-generation Languages
Intended for use by professional programmers.	May be used by a non-programming end user as well as a professional programmer.
Requires specification of how to perform tasks.	Requires specification of what task is to be performed i.e., system determines how to perform the task.
All alternatives must be specified,	Default alternatives are built in; an end user need not specify these alternatives.
Require large number of procedural instructions.	Require fewer instructions.
Code may be difficult to read, understand and maintain.	Code is easy to understand and maintain because of English-like commands.
Language developed for batch operation.	Language developed primarily for on-line use.
Can be difficult to learn.	Easy to learn.
Difficult to debug.	Easy to debug.
Typically file-oriented.	Typically database-oriented.

Merits and Demerits of 4 GLs

Although currently differing in many respects, fourth-generation programming languages have atleast following characteristics in common:

(i) **Interactive coding :** A programmer enters English-like phrases or on-screen menu choices to formulate an inquiry or define a task. Pre-written routines contained in various application packages are then invoked to enable the fourth-generation language to write its own programs in third generation languages such as COBOL or BASIC.

(ii) **Limited training required: Non procedural :** Fourth-generation languages may permit the use of familiar English verbs, nouns, and modifiers such as, "Tell me the names of all customers who have ordered J-79 robots''. Thus using 4GLs, a novice can often design a simple program, including everything from describing a data file to designing a formatted data screen with just one day of training. This is very important to businesses since 4GLs essentially allow end-users to program for themselves, thus decreasing the number of requests for formal programmer assistance. As a result, the use of fourth-generation programming languages has also been called programmers/ programming.

(iii) **Emphasis on end results :** The thrust of those languages is on specifying the dimensions of a problem rather than a complicated set of procedures with which to solve the problem. This speeds up the programming.

(iv) **Increased productivity :** With a fourth-generation programming language, just a few words accomplish much, thus enabling users to develop large systems quickly. Increases in programmer productivity of at least one order of magnitude over third-generation languages are considered normal.

(v) **Increased CPU memory requirements :** Fourth-generation programming languages require about 75% more memory than third-generation programming languages to perform the same functions. For some microcomputer users, this creates a problem.

(vi) **Faster than the third generation :** They are 10 to 100 times faster than the third generation in the time required to write a program. Author and programming language expert James Martin uses a factor of 10 as a rule of thumb for the increase in speed over the third generation. Some so-called fourth-generation languages-fall short by this criterion, but others, such as FOCUS, exceed it.

(vii) **Interpretative :** Compiled programs tend to be more efficient than interpreted programs when relatively short and simple operations are being performed on large volumes of data as they generally are in transaction processing with COBOL. When the data volume is small and the operations are long and complex, as they frequently are in decision support system applications; interpreted programs may be more efficient. Interpretative languages are often easier to debug and to extend by defining new words or functions.

(viii) **Inefficient :** It is inefficient in the use of computer resources. This is the price paid for "friendliness." The good news is that current technology is adequate for the support of fourth-generation languages and in many cases, can run a program written in a fourth-generation language with less cost than a computer of 10 years ago could run a similar program written in a third-generation language.

(ix) **No Standardization :** Fourth-generation languages are too new and too dissimilar for the purpose of categorization and standardization.

(x) It is oriented towards decision support functions, where non-programmers are more likely to be the users.

Q. : Explain some of the guidelines for procuring the hardware for library automation purpose.

Ans. Buying a computer for library and information activities is a policy decision which has to be taken by the appropriate authority. Once the decision to use a computer for library activities is taken, the next step is to study and analyse the library activities and services that can be computerised. Once this exercise is done, the next stage is to decide whether the library should have a stand-alone computer system, (i.e. a system that could operate independently) or networks computer facilities available centrally in the organization, of which the library is a part. For this purpose, the following aspects of information are necessary for the decision makers.

(i) Operations to be carried out for managing the library;

(ii) Services to be provided for the users;

(iii) Volume of data collections involved;

(iv) Number of users;

(v) Activities to be computerised; and

(vi) Service destinations.

Depending on the above items of information, the following aspects may be studied:

(1) Storage needs

— Space required for storing data.

— Access required – sequential or random access.

— External storage medium (floppies, disks, tapes, CD etc.).

— Organization of files to be stored in storage media.

— Storage space necessary for creating indexes.

(2) Devices

— Input/output devices required

— Auxiliary storage necessary

(3) Response time

The time limit for the provision of answer to the query by the system. After carefully studying the above listed aspects a suitable configuration of a computer system is proposed. Even here it is worth considering the undermentioned points for deciding a suitable configuration.

A typical configuration for a microcomputer system may be as follows :

For PCs

* IBM 300 GL (Pentium II 350) – Intel Pentium II 350 MHz (Single CPU System) /64 MB SDRAM/512 KB Cache/1.44 MB FDD/ 4.2GB Ultra DMA HDD/104 Keys Keyboard/IBM Mouse/2 PCI Slots, I ISA Slot/1 ISA/PCI Shared AGP with 4 MB Video SGRAM/ 32 BIT PCI 10 MBPS Ethernet Card/32 x CD-ROM/ Integrated Audio/1 Serial Port/ 1 Parallel Port/ 14" IBM Colour Monitor (1024 x 786 resolution) / Preloaded Window 95/98. TME 10 Netfinity, Lotus Smartsiute CD.

* IBM PC 300 GL (PENTIUM II 350) –Intel Pentium II 350 MHz (Single CPU System)/32 MB SDRAM/512 KB CACHE/1.4 MB FDD/4.2 GB ULTRA DMA HDD/104 Key Keyboard/IBM Mouse/2 PCI Slots/1 ISA Slots/1 ISA/PCI Shared AGP with 4 MB Video SGRAM/32 x CD-ROM/Integrated Audio/I Serial Ports /1 Parallel Ports/14" IBM Colour Monitor (1024x768) Resolution)/Preloaded Window 95/98, TME 10 Netfinity Netmeetings/Louts Smartsuite CD.

* Intel P-IV with Hyper-threading Techique, 2.66 GHz, FSB 800 MHz, Internal L 2 Cache 512 KB, 256 MB RAM, DDR SD RAM 33 MHz, RAM Slot-4, NIC 10/100 MBPS, Hard Disk Drive – 40 GB, ATA 150 (Enhanced IDE) 7200 RPM, INTEL 865 G Chipset, CD-ROM Drive, DVD Combo/CD-RW Drive, 1.44 FDD, 15" Colour Monitor, USB Wheel Mouse, Windows Keyboard, Windows XP with Recovery CD.

For Server

* PC Server Netfinity 3000 (8476-30U) – Pentium II 400 MHz/ 100 MHz Bus Speed/PCI /ISA Architecture /64 MB ECC DIMM RAM/512 KB Write Back Cache/1.44 MB FDD/PCI Ultra Mode SCSI Controller/9.1 GB Fast & Wide SCSI HDD/101 Keys PS/ 2 Keyboard/14" SVGA Colour Monitor (IBM) (1024 x 786)/ S3 Trio with 4 MB SGRAM (AGP on Planner)/IBM Mouse 2 Serial Ports/1 Parallel Port/1 Mouse Port/2 USB Port/32 x CD ROM / 4/8 GB HP DAT Drive (SCSI) /10/100 MBPS Ethernet Card with UTP Connector /6 Slot (32 bit PCI x 315 Ax 3)/ 6 Bays 1X330 Watt SMPS MPS/3 x Fans/ Sever Guide, Netifinity Manager, Lotus Domino (Server).
* Dual 3.0 GHz Intel Xeon Processor with 533 MHz speed, 512 KB L2 cache, 512 MB Standard/8 GB Max ECC DDR RAM with 4 bit error correction and check memory, 2x364 GB 10 K RPM Ultra 320 SCSI HDD, Integrated Raid 1 controller for Mirror ring, 1.44 MB FDD, 2x10x100x1000 Auto Sensing Ethernet NIC, CD-ROM Drive, DVD Combo/CD-RW Drive, 17 "Colour Monitor, Windows Keyboard, Optical Wheel Mouse.

Criteria for Selecting Manufacturer

After decision regarding a suitable configuration of computer system is taken, such a system has to be acquired from the market. Since there are a number of manufacturers in the computer field, the following criteria would help in selecting a suitable supplier.

— Configuration of the system offered

— Total cost of the system

— Software offered free

— Warranty period – is the warranty with spares or without spares?

— Charges for annual maintenance contract

— Number of such systems installed elsewhere by the supplier.

— Reputation of the manufacturer/and supplier.

The above factors, should be kept in mind by the purchase committee while going for purchasing a system for automation purposes.

2
Role of Computers in Library Automation

Q. : Write an essay on the history and the need of computers in libraries and the role of computers in libraries.

Or

Discussing the need and impact of computers in libraries, summaries the role of computers in libraries.

Or

Write an essay on the role of computers in libraries.

Or

Write an essay on need of computers in libraries in present time.

Or

Write an essay on computer application in library management and impact of computer technology on library services.

Ans. The growth of information has been so rapid and so extensive that users are puzzled with the problems of selection and its access. So the librarians and information professionals must be equipped to meet the challenges of the information explosion.

A computer is a machine that handles data which comprise of facts that are gathered and entered into the computer. The computer stores, retrieves, sends, receives, analyses and synthesizes the data to produce the information.

A new era of computer and other information technology have been developed to assist librarians and information workers in reaching the correct information, which provides a variety of repackaged forms of information to the user, when he requires it. The automating of library routines and services has become a common feature. Computers are not in competition with human beings, but they can be used with success in performing a variety of everyday jobs as well as being a powerful tool in information processing and dissemination. It supports the concept of paperless information society of F.W. Lancaster.

History of Computer in Libraries

The entry of computer in libraries was in the decade of 1950's. During this decade Mr. H.P. Luhan organized computerised indexing. At that time computer software were very much costly. Therefore the series of computerized indexing was in U.S.A. only. In the decade of 1960's the prices in hardware and software were reduced as a result computerised services started. In the year 1960 'American chemical society' published a journal of 'Chemical titles' with the help of computers.

In the same time there was a landmark in beginning of 'MARC-I' project by Library of Congress. In the year 1961, Mr. H.P. Luhan made a program of keyword index for the articles and its titles published in chemical abstract. In the year 1963, Mr. W.K. Gilbert prepared a report on the project-computerization by Library of Congress. In order to execute this report Library of Congress prepared MARC--Machine Readable List Catalogue. Now-a-days, different makes of MARC format, e.g., USMARC, MARC-II etc. are available.

As far as India is concerned, in the year 1965, INSDOC, computerized author and subject index of Indian Science Abstract. In the year 1967, INSDOC prepared 'Roster of Indian Scientific and Technical Translators. In addition to this, INSDOC made 'Regional union catalogue of scientific serial, Bombay and Poona. In the year 1970, it started computer communication network. Before this, the use of computer was limited up to the library premises but network changed the concept of computer use.

The deviation of libraries in having the use of computer started in the year 1980 with the availability of microcomputers. There was a library movement due to use of microcomputer as 'Intelligent terminal' in the long areas of databases mechanical control etc.

At present many libraries and information centres are using computer services which are as follows :-

1. Indian National Scientific Documentation Centre (INSDOC)

The centre started computerized services in the year 1964. First attempt was made for the collection of data for publication of union catalogue scientific periodicals. Gradually the translation services too started at the centre. After the program for Indian science abstract, was started in using key word, index, author index in FORTRAN Language, For this as on line package cyber/170/720 was developed for the purpose. Since 1975, the centre has been providing computerized SDI service.

2. Documentation Research and Training Centre, Bangalore (DRTC)

In the year 1981, DRTC started the use of computer in libraries and this centre started first SDI service and prepared its own system known as DUCFINDER. The programs of the centre are recorded in COBOL language.

The centre has developed the following programs which are as follows :-

(i) *Complete Readable Catalogue:* It is a bibliographical database and machine readable, used for information retrieval.

(ii) *Selective Dissemination of Bibliographic Information :* The centre provides the extension services of selective bibliographical information.

(iii) *Chain Index :* This part of the centre of DRTC, KWIC and POPSI indexes used for subject heading.

(iv) *POPSI :* Postulated based index was used for subjects heading and on line printer.

(v) *PROG :* In includes the work of transferred of cards and disc file.

In addition to above mentioned activities, the centre runs the project of control of serial publications, circulation control, POPSI and specific subject index.

3. Bhabha Atomic Research Centre (BARC)

The centre made on automated system for information collection and retrieval which is known as 'AFSARI'. This program is written in COBOL language.

Various types of indexing are made by the centre for example: author index, detailed and report number indexing.

4. Tata Institute of Fundamental Research (T.I.F.R.)

In the year 1970, a program based for annual acquisition in the library was made and the computers were used for information system.

5. Indian Institute of Technology, Chennai

These institutions used computer for union catalogue and abstracting of theses. It's software was written in Assemble language named as 'TEXTPAC' and it is used for SDI services of INSDOC.

6. Bharat Heavy Electrical Ltd. (B.H.E.L.)

ICL-1901 system was used. It used computer service for SDI and software in COBOL language.

7. National Informatics Centre, New Delhi (NIC)

In the year 1977, the centre was established by the Electronics Commission of India government with a view to establish information system. The centre has prepared database of the schools, higher education, informal education. scientific human power, labour welfare and employment. The centre used computer for CAS, SDI, Cataloguing. Circulation Control KWIC and KWOC indices. Its software was written in COBOL language which is known as DBMS.

8. DESIDOC

In the year 1980, DESIDOC started computerized activities with a view to provide information to scientists, engineers, industrialists for defence purposes. Its activities are as below:

(i) Subject Bibliography

(ii) Different indexing

(iii) Communication of information

(iv) Selective dissemination of information-SDI.

The package of DESIDOC was written in COBOL language and known as 'PRIME'- 750 and the package could does the following important functions:

(i) To prepare bibliographies including abstract.

(ii) To make card index.

(iii) To prepare indexing entries.

(iv) To prepare report of number of indexing.

(v) To prepare author indexing, and

(vi) To provide SDI service.

9. Indian Standard Institution, New Delhi (ISI)

Computers were used for ISI bibliographic information and managerial information. Its software was written in FORTRAN language. It prepares database to provide standardized information.

10. Steel Authority of India Limited, Ranchi

Computer is used for information mechanism. It's software was prepared in COBAL and FORTRAN language, which is for serial control, circulation control and catalouing etc.

Later, national and regional organizations like NISSAT, DELNET have shown interest in assisting the libraries by sharing their expertise by way of involving themselves directly or indirectly in the development of a software and distributing it at an affordable price. SANJAY, MAITRAYEE, DELWINDOWS are the examples of the library software which have the support of DESIDOC, NISSAT and DELNET respectively. The small libraries in particular may greatly be benefited by this gesture, as the software by these organizations is developed by experts in the field and available at relatively low prices. More recently with the advancement of information and communication technologies (ICT), it became possible to have the advanced library softwares and net working facilities.

Now the all libraries mentioned above and many more throughout the country and at International level, have advanced Library software with network systems. And these libraries are not only generating computerized services but also availing the on-line retrieval of information.

Need of Computers in Library

Libraries were in need of computers due to explosion of knowledge and information sources at one side and lack of time with the user, the other. Each library was required to provide its maximum services in least time and least cost and it made possible after the use of computers.

The following are the reasons which led libraries to make use of computer in library services :-

1. **Information Explosion :** Due to explosion of knowledge, librarians and scientists felt a difficulty of acquiring and storing

the collection of reading materials and with a view to solve this problem computer needed in libraries.

2. **Routine Work :** Computers helped in routine work like filing, typing, and other jobs of duplicative nature.

3. **Economic Feasibility :** The effect of information explosion made very costly to the printing and distribution, as a result the services provided manually became very costly. Computers helped in economize these services.

4. **Increases in Numbers of Users :** With the explosion of information the numbers of users are also increased. After Second World War there was a rapid growth in research and development. Library services slanted to new technologies like CAS and SDI services.

5. **Speed :** Computer application in library has been made essential due to its merit of excellent speed and accuracy.

6. **Repeating Jobs :** Library routine work and other technical work needs repetition and duplicacy which can be avoided with the help of computer.

7. **Resource Sharing :** With the advent of printing press and technology, there was a sudden literature explosion. Therefore no library can claim for purchasing all the book out of ocean of the knowledge and a sufficient collection for its need. Hence, a system of resource sharing and cooperation is adopted. Thus adoption of computer and resource sharing with other libraries makes easy to the library services.

8. **Organization of Information :** Due to the sudden flood in literature world has made difficult to organize and administer the library management. The almost time of library staff is consumed in technical and other routine jobs only. Under the circumstances the technical work like cataloguing and classification can be done speedily without loss to time. Now-a-days, it is available online too.

Role of Computer in Libraries

The activities which can be made automatized with the help of computer in the library, can be summed up as below :

1. Use of computer in library administration

2. Computerized services.

1. Use of Computer in Library Administration

These are the activities which are being done behind the screen and in the absence of user. As a result of computer involvement, speedy and efficient services are provided. It includes the following activities:-

(i) Administration and Maintenance

(ii) Acquisition

(iii) Serial Control

(iv) Physical Verification

(v) Circulation Control

(iv) Technical processing i.e, classification and cataloguing etc.

2. Computerized Services

Computerised services includes the following activities in a library :

(i) Current Awareness Services (CAS)

(ii) Selective Dissemination of Services (SDI)

(iii) Indexing Services.

(i) **Current Awareness Service :** C.A.S. or current awareness service, is the important service in the field of information which is given by the libraries to its readers with a view to updating the knowledge of a reader.

It includes the list of information sources with full bibliographic details like author, title, volume, pages etc. Also given subject group entry made for it and abstract. This all works are performed with the help of computer effectively.

This service is a general service, to be used by any needy readers. This service can be provided with many ways and means which is as follows :-

(a) Title announcement

(b) List of addition

(c) Content list announcement and circulation

(d) List of articles

(e) Indexing and abstracting services

(f) Digest services.

(ii) **Selective Dissemination of Information Service or S.D.I.:** This service was started in the year 1961 by Mr. M.P. Luhan. According ot Mr. Luhan its objective was to provide information and new commodities in an organization to its employees. It is the mainly computer based service. There two files are prepared to computerized this service :

(a) User file and

(b) Document file of library holdings.

If needed the changes can be made in user's file, and the file is updated by necessary changes.

(iii) **Indexing :** Indexing becomes very easy with the help of computer. To do this job, computer is given commands and directions. Thus, a separate index file is prepared without any changes in master file. Index is prepared with this help and selecting sought links of author, title publisher etc.

Impact of Technology on Libraries

The library has the opportunity to not only continue serving its user group but to expand important and relevant services to a large number of users. With the help of computers, a library is able to:

- Provide access to complicated or seldom used databases
- Provide community, conferencing and message centre program
- Provide online access to information on library resources
- Service to its community
- Provide mediated approaches to library instructions.

The impact of Computer technology can be seen as follows:

1. **Impact on Collection Development :** The impact of IT on collection development is related to several issues such as ownership vs. access, etc. Importance is given accessing the other library collection rather possessing almost all documents. Development in IT has resulted in bringing together libraries of the world at one place.

2. **Impact on Technical Services:** Computers have proven useful in handling electronic process, such as file management and supporting a variety of products from the machine readable cataloguing record, from cards to online public access catalogs.

The ease with which cataloguing records can be shared among many libraries is one of the greater benefits of library automation. OPACs can substantially reduce the cost of maintaining the catalogue. Orders may be completed by sending them electronically to vendors. Other activities aided by automation are cancellation of orders, correspondence concerning in correct or damaged items, maintenance of desirable files and monitoring vendor's performances. Fund accounting is another process greatly improved by automation and number of machine readable bibliographic tools are becoming available to libraries for use in the selection of recently published and retrospective title.

3. **Impact on User Education :** "Information literacy" is defined as, encompassing the entire world of information and seeking to prepare people to pursue the concept of life long learning. It prepares people to use information effectively. To achieve these goals, librarians and faculty will have to work together in developing teaching strategies using the latest technologies. Librarians will have to maximize the use of technology to teach more skills to greater numbers of users. It should provide basic instructions on search techniques including Boolean searching and would assure users that the system is not difficult.

4. **Impact on Reference Service :** Provision of online search services by libraries is a logical extension of traditional reference service. The reference librarian who acts as a searcher on behalf of the user has to do the following:

- Handle Client Interview.
- Interview Analysis and Identification of Information Needs.
- Translate the needs identified in the interview into various search strategies appropriate to the database selected.
- Present the result to the client.

These become easy with computer introduction.

5. **Impact on Staff**

The positive effects of library automation on the staff are –

- It reduces repetitive work.
- Upgrades the skills of the supervisory staff.
- An increase chances of getting variety of outputs from single

input and generates data.

– It can reduce the level and the quality of interpersonal communication.

6. **Impact on Information Services :** A number of computerized information services in various fields and number of large abstracting and indexing services have started producing machine readable files of large volume to suffice the purpose to give the user the right document, at the right time to the right user. These files, casually in the form of magnetic tapes, are now commercially available and can from very convenient databases for large-scale SDI services. Some of the well known services are CAS (Chemical abstract service), of ISI (Institute of scientific information), Philadelphia and INSPEC, MEDLARS, COMPENDEX. These considerable bring down the cost of input preparation and can also provide a wider coverage than what an individual system could provide.

In fact, the transformation of technology impacts on each of us personally, professionally and collectively.

Q. : What are the Computerized Information Services? Describe them briefly.

Or

Write an essay on uses of computers in Current Awareness Service (CAS) and Selective Dissemination of Information Service (SDI).

Or

What are the important components of a computerized SDI system? Discuss the significance of a user profile in providing as effective service.

Ans. Modern libraries and information centres provide a variety of documentation and information services to support R and D, industrial productivity management, marketing and trade and all other programmes of development emanating from autonomous, government and non government and academic institutions. These information services can broadly be categorized into anticipatory and responsive services. Some of the significant services which have been evolved as a result of developments in computer and communications technologies are: (1) Current Awareness Services, (2) Selective dissemination of

Information service (3) Online Search Services, (4) Printed Indexes, (5) Database Products and Services, (6) Document Delivery Services etc.

1. Current Awareness Service

Current Awareness Services play a vital role in the dissemination of information. In specialised professional fields, informal methods are used by researchers for 'current awareness'. Personal contacts, letters, and preprints of papers are used to keep each other aware of significant progress and accomplishment. This method is limited to a few and is not meant to generate comprehensive review of all activities in any subject area. This situation has led to the emergence of what is commonly referred to as current awareness service (CAS). It is varionsly defined as:

According to Strauss, it is to establish such as administration which selects the information from the available publications as well as new arrivals and also to make documentation of articles to attract the scientists. The methods, ways and means of selecting and dissemination, and information retrieval from periodicals, reports, book, patents is called "current awareness services."

According to Satyanarain and Raizada "it is such service which makes available the entire information in a easy way related with effecting research group."

CAS has also been defined as a "science – information system continually calling the scientist's attention to the newly developed material on topics falling into his longterm field of interest, which remains unchanged until further notice."

'CAS' in libraries is needed due to following reasons :-

(i) For the use of new material collected in the library.

(ii) To make available the latest reading material of their subject field to the library users.

(iii) For the best use of the documents of main sources of information.

(iv) To complete the needs of user's information.

(v) To make updated with the latest information of their subject to the users.

(vi) To save the time and labour of researchers.

Types of CAS

'CAS' can be divided into the following three categories :-

(i) International level

(ii) National level

(iii) Local level.

(i) **International level :** The objective of current awareness services at this level is to provide services to all the scientists of world related with their subject with a view to updating of their knowledge.

(ii) **National level :** The CAS provides cooperation to cater the needs of literature of research and development at national level.

(iii) **Local level:** In order to provide the service of this level includes the preparation of local documentation list. Researchers and technicians of the related institution are its readers. Their need of information can be ascertained easily.

CAS is a general service provided by the library which can be provided by many ways and means, some of them are telephone calls to individuals, (ii) recording individual references and forwarding them to the concerned persons, (iii) periodical routing, (iv) maintaining card files of references of information by manual or machine methods, (v) issuing of library bulletins, (vi) circulation of duplicated contents of periodical literature.

At present CAS is very important service which is arranged by the libraries with a view to updating of new innovations, and information science. Current awareness services contains like author, title, volume, pages etc. It also includes subject heading and if possible abstract too of an essay in its entries. The formation of the CAS can be explained as follows :-

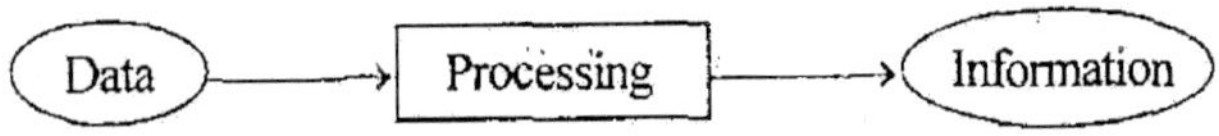

CAS appears in various forms such as title announcement, contents list, indexing and abstracting services, digest, etc. The Information Bulletin is one of the popular forms of CAS adopted by many libraries. A bulletin may be a printed list or a set list for consultation on a VDU in case on online system, which is published and disseminated among a number of user on a specific subject area. Most of the Information Bulletins, list titles or abstracts together with citations of relevant new documents in the subject area. Some bulletins offer digest of information while others actually include extracts from the documents which are announced. Usually, information bulletin is issued at regular intervals on a weekly, fortnightly and monthly basis. In some situations daily information bulletins are also issued depending upon the nature of the demand and the type of organization.

One of the most important as well as popular current awareness publications is "current contents" (life sciences, arts & humanities and also chemical sciences). This publication employs the technique of frequent gathering of title pages of journals grouped within a subjects field, which are then reproduced in the printed form and distributed prior to the arrival of the journal in the library. Journal users may scan the title pages and select the papers that should be read by them promptly. This saves a lot of time on the part of the users. Modern techniques of CAS include individual notifications of published literature in the form of Selective Dissemination of Information.

2. Selective Dissmination of Information Service

The selective Dissemination of Information Service or SDI in variously defined as under.

According to H.P. Luhan, "SDI is the service of new information provided by an institution to that parts where the possibility of its present work and tastes exists having after getting it from any resources."

According to Dr. S.R. Ranganathan, "It is the service to the readers for factual, uptodate and speedy information retrieval."

SDI was developed with a specific purpose of providing a researcher at regular intervals a carefully selected list of all publications in his particular area of interest that have been published in all the significant journals of the world in the preceding interval.

The advances in computer and communications technology and the availability of comprehensive databases covering world literature in machine-readable form including CD-ROM format, has greatly enhanced the potential of SDI Service and expanded its scope so that what was originally conceived as a local service for an individual research organization, has now acquired the function of providing a national of international service.

Components of SDI System

SDI System must have the following components:

(i) users by profiles

(ii) database or document profile

(iii) computer system (hardware)

(iv) software

(v) user and SDI system interface

(i) **User Profiles :** The clientele of the organization comprise the user community in a library for whom the SDI service is to be rendered. In fact, one of the basic steps in designing SDI service is to identify the potential users and also their subject interests and compile what is technically referred to as "user profiles". It may be mentioned that a 'user profile', is a succinct statement of information requirements of a user of group of users.

(ii) **Database :** SDI service can be offered to the users on the basis of the document resources selected and acquired by the library or the information unit. For the purpose, a computer readable database of the documentary material are acquired by the library. The database may be created with in the library i.e., in-house database. On the other hand, the library of information unit may decide to subscribe for externally created and commercially available databases on subjects of interest to the organization and search these locally with in-house computer facilities to provide the SDI service to its user community.

(iii) **Computer System :** The libraries and information units may organize SDI service either through their own database and their own computer system or could become members of a network, which can offer this facility and serve their clientele.

(iv) **Software :** There are available three option in acquiring software for SDI service.

The first option is to develop in-house software tailored to the specific requirements of the particular library or information unit, and then offer SDI service. The second one is to identify commercially available package, which could be run on the in-house computer system and provide SDI service using it. The third option is to subscribe for external databases which have a SDI software component that can be used to provide SDI service by searching that database. In the present day context the third option is more viable and financially feasible. Since software development involves a lot of money and is time consuming, the third option is more acceptable and pragmatic.

Another significant aspect worth noting in this regard is the availability of many commercial databases in CD-ROM format. Each of these has its own searchable software which may be used for SDI. But, the user profiles need to be constructed based on such software separately.

(v) **User and SDI System Interface :** Every SDI system should have a mechanism which permits interaction between the user and the system. This is essential to make the SDI service more purposeful and effective. It includes the following aspects:

(a) notification of recent literature,

(b) request to the users to furnish feed back on a regular basis. The feedback may be positive or negative depending upon the relevancy and usefulness of the items received by the user, and

(c) information intermediaries who interact with the users and are knowledgeable regarding databases, retrieval techniques, creation of user profiles, etc.

Operational Aspects of SDI

In order to provide SDI services, the following activities are performed :

– Preparation of reader's profile

– Document profile

– Matching of profiles

– Notification

– Feedback or recording of response

– Readjustment of profiles

– Responding the request of user.

SDI services can be explained and understood in a better way with the help of following diagram:

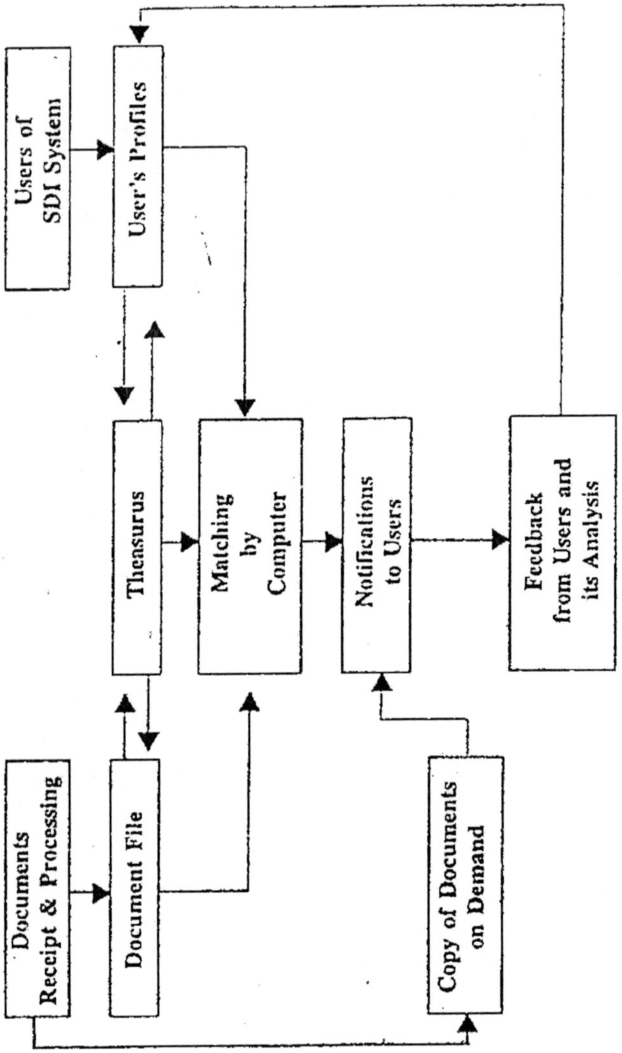
Users of SDI System
User's Profiles
Thesaurus
Matching by Computer
Notifications to Users
Feedback from Users and its Analysis
Documents Receipt & Processing
Document File
Copy of Documents on Demand

SDI – service

In order to provide SDI services by the computer, the following two files are opened:

(i) User file

(ii) Document file

These files are checked, tallied, and can be revised if needed while providing services of SDI to readers.

At present the Abstracting SDI services of INSPEC is being provided on the cards by computer printing. The same service is being provided by chemical abstracts by organizing SDI services to the persons, institutions, alongwith the uptodate references and the abstract. Canadian SDI developed by National library of Canada (CAN/SDI) is the most important progress of the field. With the help of this a cooperation can be extended to the international level. CAN/SDI services is also started by INSDOC in India with the collaboration of India Institute of Technology, Chennai.

3. **Online Search Services**

Online search service also known as online system suppliers search services, or online service spinners, are responsible for mounting databases on a computer and making the arrangements necessary for such databases to be searchable from a large number of remote user workstations or terminals. Online search service system that provide access to a large number of databases generally convert those databases into uniform format with some standardization features so that the basic commands and search techniques apply across all the databases offered by a given vendor. Naturally, the intending user needs awareness of the range of search services that are available. It might so happen that one database may be available from several search services or vendors. Access to that database may be considerably cheaper, especially once the telecommunication charges have been taken into account via one search service than the other. Moreover, a different vendor may offer search facilities which support much more effective searching for a specific topic than might be possible via another search service. Some services might offer customers other benefits such as ease of searching, processing speed and competitive pricing.

There are a number of different types of such services such as: (i) The traditional Super market online search services; (ii) Specialist online search services; (iii) Publishers as search services; (iv) Platform independent services; and (v) Bibliographic utilities.

In recent times, online service suppliers are attempting to respond to the long felt need of devising common interfaces to tools such bibliographic databases and directories including directories of Websites, which indicate the location of information and the full text of the document which contains information. Some of the sophisticated online search services are trying also to offer access to other information channels, such as databases mounted by other vendors, the contents of other Websites, information collections such as libraries, and people as information channels. This new aspect of the service is described as an Integrated Information Solution (IIS). Some of the examples of services which seek to generate integrated information solution are : (i) K R Science Base for the WWW, (ii) DIALOG Web, (iii) Engineering Information Village, etc. Such IIS need to be targeted to meet the needs of specific groups, and the service supplier must understand those needs, not only in terms of the type of the database to be accessed, but also in terms of specific features of interfaces and the most acceptable pricing strategies.

4. Printed Indexes

Computers are also used to prepare a systematic list which specifies or indicates the contents, topics, names or other information in a book or any document which are known as indexes. The computers may be used both for the preparation of in-house indexes to reports, local abstracting and indexing bulletins, patent lists, etc., and also for the production of indexes for the major abstracting and indexing journals like Chemical Abstracts, Biological Abstracts, etc. Originally, indexing was an isolated operation, but now-a-days, indexes have become one of the range of database products. Most of the indexes consist of a series of lead terms usually arranged in alphabetical order. Each lead term may be qualified and must have a link that leads the user to other lists or documents. Computer generated indexed mostly rely on automatically assigned index terms. They might also be based on intellectually or manually assigned terms.

Types of Computer Generated Indexes

There are different types of computer produced indexes, such as:

- Keyword Based Indexes
- String Manipulation Based Indexes, and
- Citation Indexes

In keyword indexes, indexes are based on keywords. KWIC, KWOC, KWIT and KWAC fall into this category. Of them, KWIC Index is the most common type of natural language indexes. It has become popular because it is straight-forward and relatively easier to produce. Generally, in basic type of keyword indexes, words in the title are compounded. A stop-list is generated and is stored in the computer memory. The stop-list contains words under which entries are not required. The use of stop-list enables suppression of the generation of useless index entries. Each word in the title is compared with those in the stop word list, and if a match occurs, it is rejected. On the other hand, if no match is found, the term is designated as a keyword. These keywords are used as entry words with one entry relating to the document for each word. The keyword is printed with the remainder terms of the title as context. Entry words are arranged alphabetically and aligned in the centre of the left column. A single line entry including the title and source reference is usually a document or abstract number. In some cases, an abbreviated journal citation may also be provided. Alternatively in some cases a full bibliographic description can be located in a separate listing. Entries under the word are arranged alphabetically by title.

In String Manipulation based Indexes, a series of terms from a controlled vocabulary of single-concept terms is chosen to represent a document then these terms are composed into an index string, which may also include delimiters which denote the way in which each term is to be treated in index entries, for example, whether it is to appear as a lead term. PRECIS, COMPASS and the index generation algorithm used in Abstracts in New Technologies and Engineering (ANTE) are the example subject indexes based on a rigid framework of conceptual analysis.

Citation indexing is one of the means of producing an effective index by the effective use of computer for arranging and reformatting entries. The input to this indexing system compresses the references of recent articles published in the core journals of any discipline. For each article, a list of works (documents) that it refers to are also compiled. In other words, a citation index lists 'cited' documents, together with a list ot those items that have cited them (i.e., citing articles). The most important example of citation indexes is that of Science Citation Index (SCI) produced by Institute of Scientific Information, Philaddphia, USA.

5. CD-ROM Database Products and services

CD-ROM is a derivation of the compact digital audio disc. All the optical formats use a set of laser pick-up optics. CD-ROM uses the digital audio compact disc (CD) system for storage and retrieval of machine-readable or digitally encoded information.

The databases presently available on CD-ROM can be grouped into the following categories:

(i) Bibliographic databases with or without abstracts, which provide access to the literature of a specific subject field or list of a type of publications such as patents;

(ii) Catalogue or book trade databases;

(iii) Source databases which contain the total contents of a documents, including as appropriate computer software, images or sound, and maps and charts, as well as any text and numeric data;

(iv) Quick reference databases which offer facts and figurers that are characteristic of directories;

(v) Mixed (i.e., databases which contain full text data) databases such as McGraw-Hill Scientific and Technical Reference Set;

(vi) Multimedia databases including databases in CD-1 CDROMXA, DVI and CDTV Formats. These products offer motion picture graphics and sound, and often the opportunity to interact with the computer.

CD-ROM database are designed in such a way that the end-user may search them without much difficulty. Many CD-ROM products offer interfaces, which enable both the novice as well as the expert user to conduct the search with ease. Retrieval facilities, generally available with any information retrieval system such as Boolean logic, truncation, product field specific searching, etc. are also provided in most of the software used for the retrieval in CD-ROM databases. The special feature of CD-ROM is the interface dialogue design.

Most products rely heavily on menus and screen prompting with windows and colour being employed to differentiate parts of the screen. Context specific help called up from a certain key has also been a feature. However, working through menus can become a chore when the user becomes more familiar with the system. Some CD-ROM disc producers have recognized this and are now providing different types of search interface with short cuts ot expert users. Installation software are also be supplied by the product producers.

6. Document Delivery Services

Document delivery is considered as one of the important elements of providing access to information. It involves the integration of document discovery, the location of a supplier, request and delivery.

It is a complex process, which spans time and distance between customer and supplier and takes many forms. For example, it may involve documents in a variety of forms and involves a number of intermediaries. In other words, document delivery involves authors, publishers, subscription agents, delivery services, book suppliers and librarians. Since information is generated in different formats, and their production involves different agencies, it is but natural that there are many options for document delivery.

The following may be the media for document delivery system.

(a) Library networks and consortia, including national libraries and document delivery services. The central focus of these network being resource sharing and the creation of shared bibliographic and catalogue database. Such agencies may also offer a range of other value-added services such as online search services.

(b) Document delivery on CD-ROM, which is particularly appropriate in the context of books, encyclopedias and other lengthy documents.

(c) Commercial Document Delivery Services, which operate with alliances with online search services and draw on the resources of a number of other libraries.

(d) Library suppliers and Serials supplier agents, who have used networks and EDI, (Electronic Data Interchange) to improve the document ordering process and associated processes such as altering invoicing and book processing.

(e) Electronic journal publishers and suppliers.

Many agencies may be involved in both electronic and print-based document delivery. Librarians, publishers and other document delivery services are concerned with the complexities of document delivery in an environment in which conventional document delivery is coupled with electronic document delivery.

Q. : Why library automation software packages needed? Explain some of the guidelines for the evaluation of software packages.

Ans. There are available a number of software packages specially designed to support various library in-house keeping operations. Some of these are integrated packages covering all functions of library, while some concentrate only on specific routines like database formation etc. The different activities of a library can be grouped as follows :-

1. Information Resource Building (IRB)

   Acquisition of monographs, Serial control including check in claiming, budgeting and subscription control; accounting and report preparation, cost modelling etc.

2. Classification and Cataloguing

   Catalogue card production and on-line cataloguing

3. Circulation control

   Book loan and Inter library loan

4. Information Retrieval

   Database creation and maintenance interactive searching of in house as well as external databases, provision of search output against specific demand.

5. Current awareness Services

   Selective Dissemination of information (SDI)

   Accession list production and

   Indexing and abstraction etc.

6. On-line search assistance
7. Training models for libraries and information users
8. Word processing application
9. Communication Network

   Electronic mail and Local area network

The library and information software sources shows that there are more software packages for database management and information retrieval than for in-house keeping routines and management support functions.

Need Library Software

There are available various software developed by different commercial organizations. Here, the question arises why we use commercially available library software rather to use own developed software. There are a number of advantages in using a commercial available software. Important ones include the following:

(i) An efficient software package requires at least 4 to 5 man years of programming effort and is very expensive to develop. The investment cost for initial creation of the package is spreaded over many users and any one user pays only part of this cost.

(ii) Since the package is to be sold, it must be viable in the market place. This implies that the package is well documented. User manuals with test data and guidance on the setting up of the systems employing the software are readily made available.

(iii) The supplier with a number of clients has sufficiently maintenance income to justify the establishment of sound service.

(iv) Packages, which have been widely used might be thoroughly tested in different environments, and thus any weakness of fault can be quickly identified and rectifed.

(v) Many desirable features are incorporated into a commercial package, which has been refined after application in several organizations, but these features may not be apparent to the user. Such features will include security pass words, back up, restart and recovery programs and integrity checking and skilled and beginner level assistance.

(vi) Existence of a user group allowing the organizations to compare it with the experience of using the package with others. This certainly provides valuable information which can be utilized for developing improved strategies for using the package more efficiently as well as for extending the use of the package to new areas.

The above mentioned aspects are the advantages relating to the use of commercial software package. But its one of the important draw-backs is that a commercial software package may have number of build in assumption about the users. For example, the educational level of the users, their expertise in handling software, etc. are of speculative nature and hence may not be correct. Software vendors may not fully be aware of the organizational philosophy of different relating to some of the packages available for automating library operations and information storage and retrieval.

Evaluation and Selection of Software Packages

The selection of a good and perfect software package is not an easy job. A package which does not perform as expected or which requires expensive modifications will shake its creditability to the librarians to purchase them. A change of finding a right package could be improved by setting up an evaluation process based on common sense, sound judgement and dash of skepticism. The most important aspects considered for the evaluation of a package are : (1) vendor or producer, (2) system output, (3) system input, (4) searching, (5) security, (6) training facility, (7) equipment, and (8) other considerations.

1. Vendor or Producer of the Package : One of the basic concerns when evaluating a software package is to know the creator or marketing agency associated with the package. Questions to be addressed in this connection include:

(i) does the vendor or producer have a reputation for reliability, responsiveness, and quality?

(ii) is the vendor a primarily library foeused agency or a general software house? The libraries have unique requirements of which non-library focused companies are not aware and therefore communication with them may need special effort.

(iii) what other products has the vendor to his credit? Are these products still in use? Do the users rate the products very high?

(iv) how many organizations have purchased this software package and what is their experience with it?

(v) what kind of support services are offered by the vendor? (i.e., installation on your own computer, debugging, conversion services, etc.).

(vi) is the vendor geographically located nearer so that he can be responsive to your questions or problem?

2. System Output : Essential to any computer-based system is the output. In other words, what the user and the library will receive from the system in response to queries. Both display on the VDU as well as printed listing capabilities must be examined. It is necessary to ensure the following aspects:

(i) is the display format easy to understand and read?

(ii) can the display format be custom tailored? (i.e. full record or specified partial record?)

(iii) can printed lists and reports be generated easily as and when required? Can they be displayed on the terminal?

(iv) can statistical reports be generated when needed?

(v) can a tape be generated as an output from the system?

3. System Input : How information is to be entered into the system using the package is one of the most essential features to be ascertained before a software package is acquired. In other words, preparation of initial input as also an ongoing procedure, it must be carefully evaluated. For this purpose, the following aspects should be considered:

(i) can MARC format be used for data input purposes?

(ii) will it be possible to choose the input means? That is to say whether we could use key to tape or key to disk as input means?

(iii) is the procedure to add new items easy? Are the commands in this regard easy to remember?

(iv) does the package have built-in-safeguards that tell us if an input error is made?

(v) can we identify without difficulty the newly input items into the system?

(vi) can deletions of entire records or partial records be made easily?

(vii) does the package allow the users to specify record structure which will meet their specific needs? Will it accept variable length records?

4. Searching Facility : Once the user creates a database or an online catalogue using the software package, he will be able to easily locate items from it. In other words, the catalogue must be searchable. In this context, it is important to look for the following aspects from the package:

(i) is the query language easy to learn and easy to use?

(ii) is there a beginning user format that explains commands in detail and an experienced user format which bypasses lengthy explanations?

(iii) if improper search language or commands are used, does the package provide for responses with intelligible error massages and alternative actions?

(iv) can all the fields in a record be made searchable or has the package any provision to make distinction between fields if desired?

(v) is there any provision to combine search terms using logical search options, AND, OR and NOT?

(vi) is the package user-friendly? In other words, can most users perform a single search such as finding a book by its author, title or a single subject.

5. Security : In case, the software package is used for the production of an online catalogue, the security of information contained in the catalogue must be ensured. In this context, it is necessary to know whether the software package possesses the under mentioned features:

(i) are there different levels of pass words of different classes of users?

(ii) if no pass words are used by borrowers, is the database secure from alteration by unauthorized users?

(iii) does the package contain any features by which the usage of the catalogue can be tracked?

If the package contains some or most of these features, then one can feel that it has normal security features built into it.

6. Training Facilities : The level and quality of training available should also be considered before a decision to purchase a software package is taken. The following aspects are to be noted in this context:

(i) are training classes for both the library and data processing staff available?

(ii) are sufficient and clear documentation and training manuals available? Are they available for librarians as well as for users?

(iii) can the uninitiated user learn to use the system? If not are there short of detailed lessons available for this purpose?

7. Equipments : Before any decision is taken to acquire a software package for any library, it is necessary to know if computer equipments are already available in the institution. In case it is available then the questions that should be asked are:

(i) can the package be used on this equipment? What operating system does the package use? Is this compatible with available hardware?

(ii) is the hardware capacious enough in terms of immediate access and secondary storage?

In some cases it may so happen that the software package is chosen first and appropriate hardware obtained later. In such a situation, some criteria such as the following be viewed so that the package can be measured against system requirement:

(i) the record format to be used, including the number of fields, the maximum number of characters per field and the number of fields per record.

(ii) the maximus number of records that the system will need to cater for.

(iii) the type of manipulations that will be required for example adding, deleting, amending, searching, sorting etc.

8. Other Considerations : Some of the other aspects to be noted are:

(i) what size of database can the package support? What are the sizes operating now and there any upward limits?

(ii) the format in which the software package is supplied. It may include disks, CDs, and tapes of varying sizes. Often a variety of formats are available but one format may be suitable for the hardware configuration to be used, and must be specified.

(iii) Besides legal factors such as warranty and contract etc. also should be clearly spelt out to avoid any future litigation.

Q. : Briefly describe the types of software packages that are useful to a library and information professional.

Ans. Computer applications to library and information sector have been one of the major factors attracting the attention of the information professionals throughout the world. In India the application of computers for library and information sector, though started in 1960s, has geared up only recently, i.e., after the introduction of computers into the market in mid 1980s. In the last two decades, several attempts were made in India at the institutional level for computerization of library and information services. Most of these efforts were piece meal and are not backed up by long term planning. However, a number of R & D organizations are now making efforts in this direction. Besides, software suppliers have realised the potential demand and also the special requirements of library and information profession and now offering software packages for the entire range of library routines from acquisitions to user education including bibliographic integrated modular software, which means that the librarian can spare the cost and effort of implementation without the risk of software incompatibility.

At present, there are more than twenty-five software packages available in India. The following table provides a list of some of them:

Software	Produced By
Archives	Minifax Electronic Systems, Mumbai
Acquas	Ober information System, Kolkata
Integrated Library Management Software	Pragati Computers Pvt. Ltd., Chennai
LIBMAN	Datapro Consultancy Services, Pune
LIBMAN	Kasban Systems Software, Chennai
LIBRA	IVV Systems Ltd., New Delhi
Golden LIBRA	INSDOC, (now NISCAIR) New Delhi
Librarian (2.1&3.1)	Soft-Aid, Pune
Library Management	Datamatics Consultants Pvt. Ltd., Mumbai
Library Management	Indo Informatics, Kolkata
Library Management	Raychan Sysmatics, Bangalore
Library Management Systems	Uandl Software Pvt. Ltd., Bangalore
Library manager	System Data Control Pvt. Ltd., Mumbai
LibSoft	ETandT Corporation, New Delhi
LibSys	LibSys Corporation, New Delhi
Listplus	Computer systems, Bangalore
MAITRAYEE	CMC, Kolkata

MECSYS	Mecon, Ranchi
NLIS	Asmita Consultants, Mumbai
SALIM	UPTRON India Ltd, New Delhi
SLIM 1.1	Algorythms, Mumbai
Tulips	Tata Unisys Ltd., Mumbai
ULISYS	Wipro Information Technology Ltd., Secunderabad
WILISYS	Wipro India, Bangalore

Study of Important Softwares

CDS/ISIS and Libsys, two softwares are most commonly used in Indian libraries. Each of them is discussed below.

CDS/ISIS Software (Micro Version)

Micro CDS/ISIS is a advanced non-numerical information storage and retrieval software package. It was developed by UNESCO in 1985 to meet out the requirements of many institutions, specially in developing countries. It is meant to facilitate streamlining of the information processing activities in developing countries with the help of relatively inexpensive modern technologies. This software was originally based on the mainframe version of CDS/ISIS started in the late 60s.

UNESCO developed version 1.0 of the software package in 1985. It was designed to run on IBM PC/XT with 256 KB RAM and hard disk capacity. Six different programs were required to execute the various functions. Version 1.0 was limited to database containing 32,000 records. In the year 1989, version 2.0 of CDS/ISIS was developed by UNESCO with integration of all programs into one and the additional advantage of extending the capacity of the database to 16,000,000 records. The special feature of this version is the introduction of the CDS/ISIS Pascal programming language interface. The CD-ROM version of the CDS/ISIS also came out in 1989.

In 1993, Version 3.0 which supports Local Area Network (LAN) was developed. Also in 1993, the development of UNIX version of CDS/ISIS became availably.

In November, 1997, version 1.0 of CDS/ISIS for Windows operating system i.e. WINISIS released. All the options of CDS/ISIS version 3.0 were available in WINISIS version 1.0 except database definition services. Hence to create a new database, one has to take help of DOS version of CDS/ISIS. The same database can be run in WINISIS. Some of the major features of WINISIS are powerful data entry option, global replacement, powerful printing format, availability of hyperlink format etc. This package also had facility for online help and online manual facility. In January 1999, the complete version of WINISIS i.e. Version 1.311 was released.

Main Features of CDS/ISIS

The main features of CDS/ISIS software may briefly by summarized as follows:

- The handling of variable length records, fields and subfields, thus saving disk space and making it possible to store greater amounts of bibliographic information.
- It comprises a databases definition component which allows the user to define the data to processed for a specific application.
- It has a data entry component which facilitates entering and modifying data through user-created database specific worksheets.
- It possesses an information component with a powerful search language providing for field level and proximity search operations, in addition to Boolean search techniques along with facilities for free-text searching.
- It has a powerful report generator facility allowing the user to create desired printed products such as catalogues, indexes, etc., according to desired formats of the users.
- It has a data interchange facility based on the ISO 2709, which is used as standard format by leading database producers.
- It has an integrated application programming language (CDS/ISIS Pascal) which allows the user to tailor the software to specific needs.
- It functions helping the user to build pseudo-relational databases.
- The package also contains an interface between the micro CDS/ISIS and the IDAMS software for statistical analysis.

Hardware and Software requirement

The requirement of hardware for different present versions of CDS/ISIS are given below:

CDS/ISIS Version	Hardware/software	Quantity
MS-DOS version	IMB PC or compatible micro–computer	1
	RAM (recommended)	640 K
	Hard Disk	2Mb
	Floppy drive	3.5 inch HDD
	Monitor (Monochrome or Color)	1
	Printer (optional)	1
	Operating System	DOS ver 3.0 or higher
Windows version	Intel 386/486 based processor at 40Mhz	1
	RAM (Minimum)	16 Mb
	Hard Disk	10 Mb
	Floppy drive	3.5 inch HDD
	Monitor (VGA 640x480 Color)	1
	Printer (optional)	1
	Operating System	Windows 3.1 or Windows 95/98 or NT
UNIX	Intel 386/486 based processor	1
	Terminal	VT 100 or compatible
	Floppy drive	3.5 inch HDD
	Screen (Monochrome or Color)	1
	Printer (optional)	1
	Operating System	UNIX system V release 3 of higher (or Linux or SCO).

Components of Micro ISIS

Micro ISIS is a set of programs written in PASCAL language. It consists of six modules to perform different functions as illustrated in figure on next page. These can be further categorized into system programs and user programs. System programs are used:

(i) to define the structure of the database, the master and index files, and the format content of the work-sheets, menus.

(ii) to reorganise, back up, and restore files.

(iii) to create message files, stop word list etc.

The end-users-that is to say librarians and library patrons are not concerned with system programs. Only database creators and managers are directly concerned with the. The end-user is the user programs:

(i) to enter and modify data

(ii) to update the index file

(iii) to search the database

(iv) to sort, display and print the results.

The user programs rely on the tables and lists of parameters specified by the data base implementation using the system programs.

Program		**Search and Data Entry**	**Menu AXGEN**
	L	– Change dialog language	
	C	– Change Database	
	E	– Data Entry	
	B	– Browse master file	
	S	– Search formulation	
	D	– Display search results	
	G	– Execute previous search	
	F	– Change display format	
	R	– Recall query formulations	
	P	– Save search results	
	X	– Exit	

Main Menu

In trying to use an information storage and retrieval software package like micro CDS/ISIS one has to know its capabilities with respect to the following aspects:

(i) data entering and modifying

(ii) indexing

(iii) searching

(iv) sorting, displaying and printing.

Micro CDS/ISIS Application

In developing a micro-ISIS application, normally the following tasks must be performed:

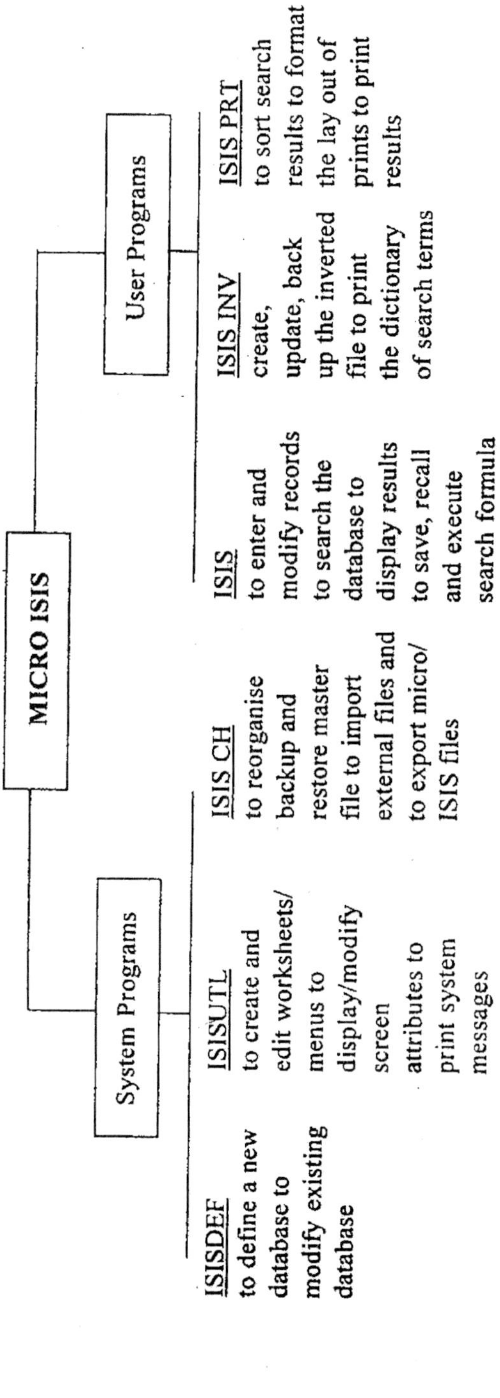

Modules of Micro ISIS

(a) Application design.

(b) database definition.

(c) data entry and indexing.

(d) searching.

For a successful implementation, the application design should be a team work of a systems analyst who knows each micro ISIS feature and knowledgeable and experienced librarian who know each specific problem of the application area. The database definition with its later modification will be performed by database manager and the daily work of record creation and maintenance certainly will be done by the library assistants associated with cataloguing division, while other library staff will be searching the database to find out some information of their requirement from the database. This implies that these tasks necessitate different competencies.

(a) Application Design : As Micro/CDS/ISIS is text oriented software package, it will be a good choice if one wished to store textual data, retrieve them by certain criteria, and display or print them in a convenient user defined format. A machine-readable library catalogue is one of the typical of its applications. All the data describing a book or any other document–are stored in the form of a record and all such records are stored in the form of a master file. In the same way we can store data pertaining to any real world entity such as plants, persons, etc. The machine-readable master file is known as a database. When designing a database, the data elements corresponding to the particular characteristics must be specified. In a bibliographical database, one can specify data elements such as:

(i) author names

(ii) titles

(iii) publication data and

(iv) subject descriptions, etc.

It is also necessary to specify which of the fields can occur in a particular database. The specification includes:

(i) a numerical identifier called tag

(ii) a descriptive name

(iii) the maximum length (field length)

(iv) an indicator for repeatability of a field

CDS/ISIS requires the fields into which a record is to be divided. It also requires specification of maximum length for a field, although that could be modified later. This package is designed to handle fields and records of varying length with a maximum record length of 4096 characters. Deciding on the field and sub-field structure of a database is a highly responsible task. One must think not only of the precise data entry and the correct printing/displaying capabilities, but also of the feasibility of the field structure for different types of searches.

(b) Database Definition : There are four basic steps involved in defining a database. They are:

(i) **Creating a Field Definition Table (FDT) :** The possible content of data records should be determined in a Field Definition Table (FDT). This table is set up by using the *Line Editor* of micro CDS/ISIS. Tag number, name maximum length, repeatability and possible sub-field identifiers are to be specified for each field.

(ii) **Creating a Data Entry Worksheet :** The default data entry worksheet is to be compiled. Worksheet editor facilities this job. Separate worksheets can be compiled to suit different requirements using the facilities of worksheet editor.

(iii) **Defining the Display/Print Formats:** A default format has to be specified. The output sequence and layout of the fields are to be described with the help of *Print Formatting Language*. This language is used throughout the system to specify field manipulations. Separate display formats can be specified as per the requirements.

(iv) **Creating the Field Selection Table (FST) :** Entering of data and creating indexes for searching is a very important feature associated with any information storage and retrieval software package. User-friendliness, reliability and data validation are the major aspects to be considered in this context. Worksheet should be defined by the system manager before any data is entered into the file. After the worksheet is created then data entry is a accomplished with the help of data entry menu. Entering and editing aspects of fields is controlled are controlled by the *Field Editor*. It provides the following features:

(i) insert and over write mode

(ii) moving cursor within a field

(iii) text deletion to the end of the field

(iv) cut and paste facilities

Program ISIS	**Database Maintenance**	**Menu AXE**
L	– Change dialogue language	
W	– Select another worksheet	
N	– Create new record	
E	– Edit record (or range)	
R	– Modify/revise last query hits	
D	– Define default values	
P	– Recall last record modified	
C	– Clair default values	
M	– Show next MFN to be assigned	
X	– End data entry	

Data Entry Menu

Moving back and forth among fields and pages of worksheet can be done on the fly. If the field is found to be erroneous, error messages and audio signals are issued by the program. Also multiple values of a field can be entered continuously if these are separated by a (%) sign.

(c) Data Entry Indexing : The CDS/ISIS package indexes all field selected for indexing into a single file. This file is known as 'inverted file'. There are indexing techniques for building index elements from lines, phrases enclosed in triangular brackets (<...>) or slashes (/...../) and from each word in the field. Non-significant words may be ignored by defining them in a stop file.

Once the new records are entered into the database, the inverted file must be updated so as to enable new records to be retrieved in searches. The CDS/ISIS allows you to select appropriate time for updating the inverted file.

(d) Searching the Database: Searching the database and printing the results of a search are important features associated with CDS/ISIS package. The query formulation strategy provided in the package uses basically Boolean logic which is enriched by proximity operators. The software allows searching only in indexed fields through FST. Searches may be stored and recalled again for display, sorting and writing to disk of printing. Saved search expressions may also be combined by using Boolean operators to further refine the searches. The search results may be output in a variety of formats by using the formatting language.

In addition to the main features, the micro CDS/ISIS package provides data exchange facilities. In other words the software package is able to accept and to produce data files applying the ISO 2709 standard format. This facility allows moving of database from one information management system to another.

Windows version of ISIS : WINISIS

WINISIS has most of the option of CDS/ISIS DOS version. The same databases created in DOS version can be used here. It has lot of additional features. Some of its advantages are given below:

1. It creates default display format.
2. It has facility to copy a record for creating a new record after slide modification.
3. Lot of formatting facilities are available like, fonts, size, colour, italic, bold, underlines etc.
4. It has facility to format the text according to the page, alignments, column etc.
5. Lot of new formats are available like-hyper linking a text file, play file, picture, Netscape file etc., calling a different display format with in format.
6. You can open a number of databases at a time.
7. It has global replacement, editing facilities.
8. WINISIS has facility to have online help message, and online manuals.

2. LIBSYS

Libsys - developed and marketed by LibSys Corporation, New Delhi is an 'integrated multi-user library information management system'. A multi-user system refers to the capability of the system to allow more than one user to have simultaneous access to the same database and to allow them to carry out the work of their choice in any module.

It is completely menu driven in all of its functions. Menus are sued to prompt the operator through the options available in each stage in the process. This design, of course, gives the novice user confidence and reduces the amount of memorising the commands or checking of manuals to a minimum.

Before using the system, the software has to be properly installed through a series of commands provided by the designers of the system. Then several default parameters as applicable to the individual libraries need to be defined for use throughout the system in various functions. These default values not only minimise the number of keystrokes during the data entry but also ensure the proper function of various modules of the system according go the individual requirements of a library. The 'System Set Up' and 'Record Keeping' options in the menu facilitate the setting up of default parameters. However, default parameters pertaining to individual module can be set from within each module also, for instance acquisition module has its own option in the menu to set up the parameters related to acquisitions process.

The Main Menu of LibSys is shown below:

Main Menu

LIBSYS

SYSTEM

Acquisition
Cataloguing
Circulation
Serial Control
Article Indexing
OPAC

HOUSE-KEEPING

System Setup
Record Keeping
Utilities

<Ret>- Select 'F10'-Quit

Main Menu of LibSys

A brief description of each of the above modules is given below:

1. Acquisition

This module basically deals with Ordering, Receipt Monitoring, Invoice Processing, Accessioning and Payment Monitoring. An updated expenditure analysis is available at any point of time.

The sequence of options provided in this module is almost in the order of the workflow involved in the activity. A brief description of the operations is furnished below:

(i) Enter Title : The first time entry of the records into the database is done through this option. The acquisition procedure begins with a search of the database to determine if the title is already in the system. No sooner is a title or a part of its entered the system checks for the duplicates. If it finds one of more matching titles all of them will be listed for perusal before proceeding further. Depending upon the situation, the operator can inform the system through function keys whether the title to be entered in is new title or a duplicate copy of the title to be acquired or different editions of the same title are to be acquired. In the latter case, the necessary bibliographic details will however, be copied from the already available records, and thus save the sata entry time. If the title is new, the system provides a data entry screen in which the data needs to be entered.

(ii) Ordering: Ordering is quite simple in LibSys. An order is to be established by including those titles that have either been approved or those for which approval is not required. The order for material received 'On approval' is prepared separately than that for other requested titles for which a firm order is placed. Prior to processing an order, the details can be modified, more titles can be included or existing ones can be removed.

(iii) Receiving : There is a simple procedure to record the details of items received against an order. On selection of this function from the menu, the system asks for the order number against which this item has been received. The system keeps track of the number of titles ordered and number of titles received. It is possible to generate claims for titles which have not been received.

(iv) Invoice Processing/Accessioning: The details of the invoice received by the library needs to be entered. The system allows for more than one invoice for an order. However, the system keeps an updated status of each order with respect to titles Ordered, Received and Accessioned. During accessioning work, the unit price, discount, exchange rate etc., can be amended if required. The system not only convects the price into Indian currency but also computes automatically the total amount of the invoice being entered. One of the features of LibSys is that the system can be set to generate the accession numbers automatically. Further, different series of accession numbers can be maintained. Once a title is accessioned, the data will automatically be available for cataloguing.

(v) Payment Processing : When an invoice amount matches with the gross total cast of each item accessioned against it, the invoice can be processed for payment. The payment processing work involves preparing a requisition form for the accounts department to process the bill and prepare the cheque. The system also helps in recording the payment details such as cheque number, bank name, amount and date of cheque, etc.

(vi) Other Modules : The 'Record keeping' module under the Acquisition sub-menu helps to maintain updated records of vendors, budget heads, currencies, yearly budgets, exchange rates and various texts to be included in different reports produced by the system.

The 'Enquiries' option provide information about various activities under acquisition. For instance, at any point of time, one can know the status of an item under acquisition or an order or an invoice.

The 'Reports' option, on the other hand, is used to get hard copy (printed copy) output from the system. To mention a few, the LibSys system can print Purchase Order, Claim Notices, Accession Register and Vendor Directory etc.

It is important to note that there is a separate module for acquiring the books received as gifts.

2. Serials Control

The serial system of LibSys provides control of periodical subscription and subsequent monitoring of the scheduled arrival of individual issues. It maintains a record of budget sanction for serial under different categories, amount unnumbered and expended, and thus providing complete budgetary control. The system is capable of handling serial which may be received on gratis or exchange basis.

The modules under Serial Control include New Subscription, Renewal, Invoice Processing, Receiving Issues, Issues Monitoring, Claims Monitoring, Bindery Management, Circulation of Serial Issues, Article Indexing, Enquiries, Reports, Records Keeping, System Set-up and housekeeping. A brief description of the major modules is described here.

(i) New Subscription : The subscription process for a new serial is initiated by entering its details and starting subscription year. The journal's name, publisher, country of publication and starting subscription year are the pieces of information which are mandatory and must be entered to initiate the subscription process of a new serial. If a specimen copy is required before actually subscribing, the second option in the sub-menu under new-subscription needs to be invoked.

Once the approval procedure is completed, the formal order for the journal subscription may be sent using the options 'Ordering'. The ordering procedure in this module is similar to that of the ordering procedure in acquisition module.

(ii) Subscription Renewal: This is almost similar to that of a new-subscription excepting that the details of the journal need not be entered. However, if there is any change in the subscription rates or other details, it can be amended in the existing records. The approval process and ordering, however, remains the same as that in case of a new subscription.

(iii) Invoice Processing : The processing of invoices include the entering of invoice details, payment requisition and payment cheques updates. The processes are similar to processing of invoices in acquisition module.

(iv) Receiving : There is a simple procedure to record issues of serials received from time to time depending upon their frequency. System keeps an updated record of the holdings of these received issues. There are different functions for recording the regular issues and index issues.

(v) Claims Monitoring : The monitoring of issues to be received as per the respective frequency of each subscribed serial, basically involves generating notices which could be mailed directly to the vendors/ publishers for 'overdue', 'not received', and 'received soiled/ damaged' issues.

(vi) Bindery Management : One of the positive features of LibSys is that it supports the bindery management. On demand the system is capable of identifying completed volumes which can be sent for binding. Further, it also supports generating bindery orders and also receiving them back to the library.

(vii) Article Indexing : One unique feature of LibSys is that it provides a facility for article indexing. Specialized services such as SDI and compilation of bibliographies can be derived from this article database.

(viii) Other Modules : The basic purpose of modules like 'Records Keeping', 'Enquiries', 'Reports', System Set-up' and 'Housekeeping' are the same as in the 'Acquisition function'.

3. Circulation

The circulation system of LibSys maintains updated membership records as well as the latest status of collection meant for circulation. The system performs all the usual functions related to circulation providing suitable validity checks at every stage. The system also takes care of infrequent but routine functions such as bindery record management and display of recent additions etc.

The major modules under the Circulation are Membership, Records Monitoring, Issues, Return, Reservation, Reissue, Recall, Inter-Library Loan, Enquiries, Reports, System Set-up, Housekeeping, Serial Circulating and Fine Collection. Circulation is one of the simplest routines to operate in LibSys. Membership Records module enables registration, cancellation, and modification of membership status of library users. Different categories of members having varied borrowing privileges can be maintained. Similarly, different categories of items having varied loan periods can be defined in LibSys.

(i) Issues/Return : Checking out of document is initiated by entering the valid borrower's identification number (membership number) and document identification number (usually, accession number). If the document to be borrowed is not in the database at the check out time, the system automatically provides a data screen to enter the bibliographical details of the document. Checking in is a simple and straight forward operation. Inputting document identification number invokes the process by displaying the details of the borrower. The system waits for the confirmation by way of pressing <Enter> key from the operator to proceed further. This is a good feature as it helps in avoiding faulty check in of some other item. In anycase, the operator has to be careful to check the details before confirming to the system.

(ii) Renewal, Reservation and Recall : There is a provision to renew an overdue document unless it is not reserved. It is interesting to note that the number of times an item may be reissued can also be controlled by setting the system suitably.

Reservation of borrowed document is allowed in LibSys. One good feature of the system is that the reservation can be made either at copy specific level or title specific level. Once the document on reserve is returned a suitable message will be displayed and the system can produce a notice to the concerned member about the availability of the item for borrowing.

The system can also maintain a reservation queue and proper monitoring of it is done automatically. The system allows recalling a document. Besides, routine recall of overdue material by issuance of overdue notices, the system also provides the facility to recall on demand any loaned document.

(iii) Enquiries / Reports : The circulation related enquiries and statistics could be derived from the system with a few keystrokes. As may be noted from the earlier modules also, in LibSys enquiries provide information on the screen and a report gives the information in a printed format. Subject wise, Member Category wise, hourly circulation statistics are available at any point of time. It is needless to say that these kinds of statistics go a long way in decision making by the library manager.

One unique feature in the circulation module is that the system records the staff identification number by way of LibSys login account ID for all the transactions. Further, LibSys ensures unauthorized persons. Thus, it is possible to identify the person who has carried out a transaction in circulation.

(iv) Record keeping, Housekeeping and System Set-up : As in earlier modules in Acquisition and Serials Control, these modules help in routine database management work and system parameter setup related to circulation activity.

4. Cataloguing

This module basically allows one to-input cataloguing details into the records created in acquisition, to accept data in standard formats such as CCF, ISO-2709 MARC, etc; to update the database through retrospective conversion for the items not acquired through the system, to derive specialized services such as CAS, SDI, Bibliographies, etc, and to export data into standard formats. Some features of this cataloguing function are briefly described here:

(i) Maintenance : Database updating such as addition, modification and removal function is done through this module. Once an item is accessioned, the record will automatically be available for cataloguing purpose. The cataloguing entries such as Class Numbers, Added Entries, Keywords etc., need to be added and the item has to be identified with an appropriate category such as for circulation, 'for reference', 'for textbooks', and so on. Based on the category defined here, an item's borrowing conditions are established. It can be noted here that until an item is passed through this module, the system does not allow its circulation.

Retrospective conversion option under this module helps in entering the details of those documents that have been acquired and processed before the system is actually installed. A few other options such as 'Update holdings', 'Change Accession Number', Change Document Type', etc., gave been provided to set right the inconsistencies that might be there in the entries.'

(ii) Other Modules : As mentioned earlier, user specific services can be derived out of the system. These include 'New Arrival List', 'CAS', 'SDI', 'Book Arrival Notices', 'Bibliographies', etc. Further as in other modules, there are options such as 'Housekeeping', 'Record Keeping', Enquiries', 'Reports', etc.

5. OPAC (Online Public Access Catalogue)

LibSys has a powerful and user-friendly search module. In a multi-user environment, a terminal could be dedicated to the public so that they could interact with the system themselves. LibSys provides suitable and sufficient security to ensure that the users are given only read-only access to the database. Further, it is possible to define the databases that can be thrown open to the public for consultation. An online help provided by the system makes the system, more user-friendly and interactive.

The database can be searched virtually by any field. However, in the interest of memory conservation and speed of retrieval, it is advisable to define only important fields such as author, title, etc., as searchable ones. The menu options provided under OPAC allow searching, the database mainly under Author, Title, Class Number, and subject.

3

Computerized Services : Library Administrative Services and Information Services

Q. : What do you mean by computer? What are the uses of computers in library administration?

Or

How much types of computers there are? Write an essay on Computer based library services.

Or

Write an essay on use of the computers in Circulation Control and Serial Control.

Or

Write an essay on computer application in libraries.

Or

Write an essay on antomation of various in-house keeping library operations.

Or

Discuss the significant aspects relating to the computerization of a serial control system in a library.

Ans. Computer is defined as an electronic machine with some mechanical facilities and is mainly needed for data processing. It performs the arithmetical and logical operations on input data and gives the desired output.

A modern computer consist of Input Devices, Central Processing

Unit (CPU) and output devices. Through input devices, data are feeded into computer, in CPU all operations take place and through output devices, desired results are obtained.

Types of computers

On the basis of operations and capacity, the computers may be:

- Analog computers
- Digital computers and
- Hybrid computers

1.Analog Computers : The name "analog" comes from the word "analogues", meaning "similar". For instance the thermometer, records various mercury levels based on changes in temperature. In other words, changes in temperature are shown by analogues changes in the level of mercury. Similarly the analog computer, converts data into voltages and computes by measuring the changes in voltages. Thus, as a measuring device, it represents values by continuously varying physical data such as the amount of pressure, voltage, or electric current. Computations are performed by combining these quantities.

Analog computers are commonly used in process measurements in industries, such as chemical and electric power plants, and petroleum refineries. Their primary advantage is prompt response to the handling of data generated by an ongoing physical process.

2. Digital Computers : In a digital computer, all arithmetic computations depend ultimately on counting. Unlike the analog computer, which receives data in a continuous form, the digital computer handles numbers in discrete from. It is capable of reading numbers in degrees of accuracy far greater than those reached by the analog computer. In addition to arithmetic operations, it edits input data, and prints out the results of its processing at high speed. Although the analog computer has similar characteristics, the method of accomplishing them is very different and cumbersome for business applications.

Digital computers are used in handling business applications, when repetitive routine arithmetic operations are involved and when hundred percent accuracy is demanded.

3. Hybrid Computers : A Hybrid computer, combines the measuring capabilities of an analog computer and the logical and control capabilities of the digital computer. It offers an efficient and economical method of working out special types of problems in science and various areas of engineering. Among the applications are space vehicle simulations and the training of space pilots, analysis of signals received from special sensor attached to humans and animals in laboratories, and the solving differential equations for chemical reactors.

Where as, on the of speed, word length and memory, the computers may be:

- Micro-computers
- Mini - computers
- Mainframe computers and
- Super - computers

1. Micro-computers: The microcomputer gets its name from the fact that its main computing component, the microprocessor, is located on one integrated circuit or chip. Larger computers use more than one chip for the various processing components. Microcomputers fit nicely on desktops; for that reason they are sometimes known as desktop computers. Many individuals purchase microcomputers for personal use, either for their jobs or for other purposes. Micro-computers then are also known as 'personal computers'.

Example : Apple, Microsomes and IBM PC and its compatibles.

2. Minicomputers : Minicomputers, more popularly called medium-sized computers, are smaller, slower, and less expensive than mainframes. They have no special power or environmental control requirements, so they can be located conveniently throughout an organization's facilities. They can perform many of the tasks that a mainframe can, but on a reduced scale. They can support a network of user terminals, but not as many as mainframes can. They can store and retrieve data from the same types of input and output devices as mainframes, but have a smaller storage capacity.

Example: HP-3000, PDP-8, Omega 58000

3. Mainframe Computers : Mainframes make up the bulk of computer installations in large organizations at least in the sense that they do more day processing work than any other types of computers. They have special power and environmental control requirements, and are housed in special rooms. This features has added greatly to the mystique of computing.

Mainframe computers often serve more than one user at a time because they are able to support large networks of individual terminals and remote job-entry locations. Most professional programmers work in a mainframe environment, preparing new programs and maintaining existing ones.

Example : Cyber 170, IBM 360/370

4. Supercomputers : The present day supercomputers are about 50,000 times faster than a typical microcomputer. They are required by certain research laboratories and for computing tasks of huge magnitude as involved in oil exploration, worldwide weather forecasting and weapons development. They are also needed for further research in 'artificial intelligence' i.e., simulation of human intelligence by learning, reasoning, adapting or self-correcting, and its by-product, the development of large 'expert systems'.

Example : Crayer of America and NEC of Japan

Computer Applications in Library Administration

International Encyclopaedia of Information and Library Science defines Library Automation as 'the use of automatic and semiautomatic data processing machines to perform, such as traditional library activities acquisition, cataloguing and circulation. Although these activities are not necessarily performed in traditional ways, the activities themselves are those traditionally associated with libraries; library automation may thus be distinguished from related fields such as information retrieval, automatic indexing and abstracting and automatic text analysis.

Broadly speaking, the activities and processing of services, which are performed in the absence of users or activities of library staff behind the screen is included in administration of library. Effective library services are being provided through these activities as an administration. It includes the following activities:

1. Administration and maintenance
2. Acquisition
3. Serial control
4. Physical verification
5. Circulation control
6. Technical processing

1. Administration and Maintenance

With the application of computer services in a library, efficiency and improvement can be achieved. Computers can help in processing data speedily. The following administrative activities in a library can be performed with the help of computers effectiviely:

(i) prepareing the reports of the meetings,

(ii) makeing copies of library rules,

(iii) maintaining record of leave of library staff,

(iv) maintaining filing and registers of administrative orders.

Thus, with the help of computer in a library much administrative jobs can be performed in a least time and optimum cost.

2. Acquisition

A rich collection of a library makes it glorious, as the entire services depend on it. After a rational book selection the first step starts for placing the order and acquisition of reading material. Mainly acquisition includes book selection, book order and acquisition.

Any automated library should follow up the points mentioned below for acquisition process:-

(i) To collect the suggestion of users,

(ii) Should prepare a list for final approval of library committee,

(iii) To send the order for the books to be acquired,

(iv) To prepare and maintain accounts of acquired books and to make preparation of payment,

(v) Statistics and accounts to book budget,

(vi) To watch and see that whether supplier is supplying book in proper order and the terms and conditions of discount and F.O.R. facilities.

A computer based acquisition system involves at least following files.

(A) Holding file : This file denotes for library documents and catalogue.

(B) Order file : It includes order number, bibliographical details main list and budget etc.

(C) Suppler file : It records the detailed information of the books listing and other bibliographical details of the needed publications by the users.

(D) **Fund file :** It keeps the subjectwise allocated amount of library budget.

(E) **Currency file :** It keeps the record of the details of the book and accession number.

Thus, with the help of computer the works related with acquisition can be processed with more speedier.

3. Serial Control

It is very essential to keep the record of reference section to get and receipt record of periodicals, its complete documentary record, and availability of the serial numbers available. It is very difficult work. How many periodicals are subscribed in a library and how many issues are published? Serial publications include journals, newspapers, annual reports, progress series, proceedings of learned body etc.

Serial control means to frame policies, methods, and execution of process by which acquisition of them can be performed. Serial control includes the following activities:

(i) To make input entry of serial data.

(ii) To maintain record of newly subscribed periodicals and its receipt record.

(iii) To get knowledge whether the up-to-date record is maintained for incoming periodicals.

(iv) To make list of the lost serial.

(v) To send reminder to the vendor for non receipt of periodicals.

(vi) To maintain the record of payment.

(vii) To prepare the slip for periodical.

(viii) To make updating of periodical list.

To get the work done, a bibliographical detail should be prepared and files should be opened as follows:-

(a) User File : As selection of the serials is mainly based on the recommendations of the subject experts both in special and academic libraries and to some extent in public libraries as well. Many of the systems have a user file. The users are given unique user numbers which form the chief source for identification of the file. The file contains the following data:

(i) User name

(ii) Address

(iii) Telephone number etc.

(b) Master file : A master serials file is to be created with the journals to be subscribed during the current year. The master file generally includes:

(i) Supplier file.

(ii) Serial file.

(iii) Order file

(iv) User file

A *supplier file* should *generally* have the following data elements:

(i) supplier number

(ii) Supplier name

(iii) Address

(iv) Telephone number

(v) Telex number

(vi) Cable/Gram

(vii) Currency

A *serial file generally* comprises the following data elements:

(i) Journal code

(ii) Title

(iii) Volume number

(iv) Issue number

(v) year

(vi) Publisher

(vii) Address of the publisher

(viii) Price (both in Indian and foreign currency)

(ix) Paid amount

(x) Cheque number

(xi) Supplier number

(xii) Expected commencement date

(xiii) Code to indicate whether it is a new order or a renewal.

(xiv) User number.

The titles of serials are subject to change and attempts have been made to provide a unique code for each serial title. One such system is CODEN which is a six character alpha-number code. The second one is the ISSN (International Standard Serial Number). These are eight digit numbers. They are extensively used as journal codes.

The *order file* has order details covering:

(i) Order date

(ii) Order number

(iii) Order information (as in Serial File)

The output of manipulated *Master* File are:

(i) Updated Master File and

(ii) Order letters

The Master File is generally maintained on tape.

(c) Fund file: It keeps the record of available fund i.e. Receipts and payment and budgetary provisions.

(d) Accession File : In certain systems a separate Accession File is maintained which holds details like:

(i) Date of receipt

(ii) Supplier number

(iii) Journal code

(iv) Volume and issue number

(v) Subscription

(e) Supplier file: It keeps the record of Agents and publishers.

(f) Receipt file: The periodicals received on exchange basis are kept in this file.

(g) Binding File or Master holding file: The various issues are to be bound on completion of the volume. A separate Binding File is maintained in some of the computer based systems. Such a file generally includes the following data elements:

(i) Journal code

(ii) Binder's number

(iii) Binder's address

(iv) Estimated cost

(v) Actual cost paid

(vi) Style of binding.

Periodically the computer can alert the serial librarian about the completion of a vclume and print such a list. This list will be the list of journal volumes that are to be sent for binding.

The computer can also be used to generate bindery notices with a detailed set of instructions to the binder.

(h) Index file : It is the record of all the indexed periodicals for research approach and purposes. After preparing the file, serial control are performed with more speedier.

Title name of the periodical, publisher with its full bibliographical details are entered in input of the computer in a specific period with a view to forecast how many periodicals are received and reminders shall be given for non-receipt of journals. If not received, vendor shall be reminded and thus an accession list (uptodate) shall be prepared for use. Thus, computer can control serial publications very easily.

4. Physical Verification

Earlier the work of physical verification was regarded as a tiklish job and not so important as it is against the principles of library science as it is an obstacle for free use of library.

Today library stock verification work is not important because the spirit of the principles of library science is 'Every reader should be provided its book'. Though some readers come in the library to steal the books, pilferaging the pages at one side and being a growing organism, the other is a situation where stock verification of a library is not possible in a certain period of intervals.

Now it is being done with the help of computer. Accession numbers from beginning number to last are entered as the input in computer. Then the numbered book available in the library including issued are recorded. Also the book in technical section for processing, sent for binding, inter library loan, the entire information is entered in the computer. The List A (total accession numbers) is tallied with the books available and a list of non available book is prepared.

Thus, library stock verification is being done for keeping record. In the same time a separate list is prepared for unused, torn and to be weeded out books.

5. Circulation Control

The circulation is the main function of a library and quite laborious too. This work can also be done efficiently and speedily with the computers. Circulation work should perform the following functions:

(i) Provision of information on the location of circulating items– either all items or only those items on loan or elsewhere, i.e. at the bindery, on reserve, being recatalogued, etc.

(ii) Identification of items on loan to a particular borrower or class of borrowers (namely, off-campus users).

(iii) Recording of *hold or personal reserves* for items on loan but desired by another borrower, often with additional provision for notifying the library staff when the item is returned and printing a book available notice for mailing to the person who requested the item.

(iv) Printing recall notices for items on long-term loan.

(v) Renewal of loans.

(vi) Notification to the library staff of overdue items and printing of overdue notices.

(vii) Notification to the library staff or problem borrowers i.e., those with unpaid fines, or overdue books, either at the time of an attempted loan or at the time a borrower is leaving the institution or on request from the library.

(viii) Calulation of fines, printing of fine notices, recording receipt of fines, and sometimes printing of fine receipts.

(ix) Calculation and printing of statistics of various types.

(x) Analysis of both summary statistics and statistics for the circulation of particular items for use in acquisition, planning of service and for other administrative purposes.

(xi) Provision for handing special categories of borrowers and special types of materials, and

(xii) Provision for printing due date slips, automatically generating orders for lost books or additional copies and printing mailing labels for remote borrowers.

To get the works done as above, the following files shall be opened :

(a) Transaction file : The transaction file contains records of all books currently on loan. This file also included books on inter-library loan, on display, in binding, etc. This file covers information about documents, borrowers and date.

(b) Document file : The document file contains information about:

(i) Document identification number (DIN),

(ii) Author(s),

(iii) Title,

(iv) Edition (if any),

(v) Volume (if multi-volumed),

(vi) Year of publication,

(vii) Name of the publisher,

(viii) Place of publication, etc.

The DIN can be any one of the following:

(i) Call number,

(ii) Accession number,

(iii) Alphabetic random code,

(iv) ISBN and copy number,

(v) Random number, and

(vi) Any other locally structured number.

The bibliographical details about a document are recorded in two ways:

(i) By absence system

(ii) By inventory system

Absence System : The information about a document is added whenever it is charged. In other words, we can say that, in this system the file contains information about those documents that are loaned out.

Inventory System : The file contains full bibliographical details of all the items held by the library.

In an absence system, generally there are less bibliographical details, whereas an inventory system can have more bibliographical details. The inventory system requires a large file capacity and it thus uneconomical.

(c) Reader file : It records the detailed information of user reader like–syllabus number, name of reader, address of reader and registration number of reader etc.

The work of computer becomes more easy with the help of these files of circulation. Every reader is provided a bar Code-Card containing the full information of the reader. In the same way another Bar coded card is prepared for every book. While making issuance of book to the reader it is examined whether number of books to be issued to the member is completed or remains due, if the number, of books are taken sufficient no further issue is made feasible or he/she shall be issued if number of limit is not crossed. This entire information is transferred to central processing unit where the entire information is stored. At the time of returning book, the due date of returning is known and book is returned with or without charging fine as the case may be.

Thus, with the help of computer circulation work can be performed in a better way.

6. Technical Processing

'Technical processing' means for classification and cataloguing work in a library which can be understood as follows :

(A) Classification : Classification by the computer has its own limitations. Therefore appropriate class number is decided for a particular book and the number is entered the computer though book can be arranged according to the accession numbers of the books but it will not be in helpful sequence.

Separate programs are made for different schemes of classification. The System Development Corporation, California, USA investigated the application of factor analysis to problems of document classification. Factor analysis is a mathematical technique for deriving classification categories for a set of documents. A computer program prepares the document-term matrix for input to the factor analysis program. The incidence on term, and association among terms are computed. Finally, the classification categories are derived on the basis of this study.

Neelameghan and Venkatraman conducted experiments in India in 1968 on the synthesis of class number by computer in which kernel terms expressing a subject in the natural language are given. For this study the Colon Classification (CC) of Ranganathan was used.

This study was divided into the following phases:

- Preparation of the CC schedule on tape;
- Reading in Kernel terms;
- Distribution of Kernel terms;
- Synthesizing the class number; and
- Printing out the class number;

In each of the schedules, the isolates are enumerated with the appropriate connecting digit prefixed to it. The isolates in the schedule are given in the inverted sequence, i.e., the sequence in which they will appear in the synthesized class number. A few synonymous and near synonymous terms for certain isolates may be given in the schedule. Such a schedule is put on a magnetic tape.

The Kernel terms, in random sequence, with the bibliographical specification of the host document are punched on cards and read by the machine. The machine compares each of the Basic Class terms and isolate terms with each of the kernel terms fed in starting from the beginning of the schedule. The machine will scan the various kernel terms in the schedule in the facet sequence. Whenever there is a match, it will pick up the number against the term along with the prefixed connecting digit. The first term to be translated is always the Basic Class. It has bo prefixed connecting digit. The machine successively scans the schedules until the corresponding isolate number for all the Kernel terms have been picked up and assembled to form the class number. Special programs have been prepared to represent the devised isolates in CC class number.

The TIFR library is maintaining a computerized classified catalogue where entries are arranged according to the UDC scheme. The class number is being used for on-line search.

(B) Cataloguing : Cataloguing includes the job of describing, recording and displaying details of the holdings of the library.

The major objectives for automation support to cataloguing are:

(a) To speed up the processing of materials into the collection;

(b) To reduce the clerical effort, stationary (such as work sheets, cards etc.) and unit cost of cataloguing a work; and

(c) To act as a common means to library materials across libraries.

Computers are used to aid in the production, maintenance and updating of catalogues.

In order to get this work done the following files are to be opened :

(i) **Master file :** It is made after making few additions and alterations in book receipt file.

(ii) **Index file:** This file contains the different entries like author, heading and subject as an information.

(iii) **Authority file :** Publisher, institution, language etc. are entered in the file for information retrieval.

Thus, the use of computer saves the time to be consumed in classification and cataloguing, while in manual readers remain without use of book as the maximum time of library staff is consumed in cataloguing and classification.

Q. : What do you menu by Library Automation ? why it is necessary? Discuss the essentials of library automation with its planning.

Ans. The term automation was first introduced by D.S. Harder in 1936. He defined it as the automatic handling of parts between progressive production processes in relation to engineering industries. Since then the term has been applied to a wide variety of automatic machinery and automatic systems; and is commentry used to describe any operation in which there has been a substantial substitution of controlled action for human efforts or intelligence.

As far as the library antomation is concerned, it is the use of automatic and semi-automatic data processing machines to perform such traditional library activities as acquisition, cataloguing and circulation. Although, these activities are not necessarily performed in traditional ways, the in-house activities themselves are traditionally associated with libraries. Library automation may be distinguished from related fields such as information retrieval, automatic indexing and abstracting and automatic textual analysis.

In an automated library operation environment, staffs and computer share the responsibility for performing work. For example, a staff member might perform the first five processing steps; the computer the next 20 steps; the staff member the next three operations and so on. Thus, in any automated library operation human beings are assisted by a computer to accomplish the work.

Need for Library Automation

Computers have revolutionized all fields of knowledge and have been gradually weaving electronic webs in various parts of the globe for quite a few years. Now it is being used extensively in libraries by developed countries and in the third world countries as well.

The need for automation is emphasized because of the following factors:

(i) Traditional methods for handling the information are inadequate as information is becoming bulky and growth rate of information is high.

(ii) Difficulty to update the information due to voluminous increase and rise in the degree of specialization involved.

(iii) Techniques are suggested for applying the computers with its advantage of speed, vast storage capacity and accuracy to library work.

(iv) The need for co-operation and resource sharing and hope of achieving some saving through automation made to switch over to automation.

(v) Operational advantages:

   (a) Offer flexibility.

   (b) Speeds up processing.

   (c) Greater accuracy, efficiency, consistency and improved work control.

   (d) Reduces repetitive clerical work.

   (e) Permits case of bibliographic control, checking and updating.

   (f) Permits improved budget control.

Essentials for the automation

The essential things for the library automation include -

(i) Good collection

(ii) Finance

(iii) Computer hardware

(iv) Computer software

(v) Staff training and

(vi) User training

(i) Good Collection : Computerization is not just for the sake of computerization, rather it is meant to serve the users with better library services and to provide access to information. For this purpose, first of all the collection of the library should be good and tolerably comprehensive. If the collection is not good what is the use of automation?

For e.g., the university library should have a book acquisition policy and norms for building up of a good collection. Collection building is a much more difficult task than purchasing a computer system. Computer can supplement and enhance the quality of the library collection but it cannot altogether replace the library collection. Hence every library should aim at the good collection building first and computerize the library collection and its services next. The good collection of the university library is the intellectual barometer which attracts teachers, students and the scholars.

(ii) Finance : Finance is the backbone of any venture. UGC norms stipulate that the university library be allocated 10% of the university budget. This rule is followed more in violation. Finances are required in the university library for

(a) Collection building

(b) Computer system

(c) Recurring expenditure

For collection building, every university in view of the rising costs of reading materials and the declining purchasing value of rupee, should provide at least 15% of the university budget annually. Then only it can be felt that the university administration is really interested in the university library. Secondly, the university library would require a minimum non-recurring amount of Rs. 10-12 lakhs for establishing a computer system. Thirdly, the university library would need an amount of Rs. 3 to 5 lakhs annually for the maintenance of the computer system and its updating and uninterrupted power supply etc.

(iii) Computer Hardware : Selection and purchase of a computer system is a complex procedure. The university library should decide first what type of computer system will be needed for its work. There are variety of computers and computer makers.

A university library would require a computer system rather than a single PC. In computer systems there are LAN, WAN, etc. A university library would at least require a LAN with facilities for e-mail and Internet. There are different types of firms and organizations which supply computer hardware and parts such as:

- Computer manufactures
- Independent terminal and peripheral manufactures
- Selling companies
- Brokers
- Leasing companies
- Retail shops

There are many computer manufacturers such as Compaq, IBM, Macintosh, Apple, UNIX, Wipro and HCL etc. compaq, Standardization in the hardware is an important factor. Otherwise it would become obsolete in no time. Fast changes are taking place in this area. Hence the librarians have to be cautious and think seriously before they decide about the computer hardware.

(iv) **Computer Software** : Computer softwares are generally expensive but a good software must include:

- utilities/format conversion programmes
- application software
- database management system and data dictionary software
- data communication software
- programming aids and testing aids etc
- additional system software

A software is generally invisible and unverifiable till it is acquired and used in the library. There are many library software packages today in the market. Some of them are CDS/ISIS. WHIZKID, TULIPS, LIBSYS, LIBRIS, OASIS, BASIC PLUS, TECHLIB plus etc.

Planning of Library Automation

An automated library activity results when a computer is used to support a library such as acquisition, processing, circulation of materials or provide access to information.

While planning for library automation, following factors should be kept in mind.

(i) **Aim : First component of automation is its aim, the purpose, the** reason, why the set of library activities are to the organized. This aim will be the focal point for integrating automation into the activities and for operating and managing the activities after automation.

(ii) **Processing :** Second component is the processing consisting of step by step operations performed in an orderly and pre-determined sequence on information materials or other items to achieve the desired result or service. The vendor of the computer system may assist in translating the library's practices and procedures during series of discussions.

(iii) **Computer system :** The third component is the computer system supporting the activities. The supporting computer may be a micro-computer, a mini computer or a mainframe. Its size may depend upon -

(a) The nature of functions to be automated.

(b) The number of functions to be supported by the computer.

(c) The anticipated volume of processing activity.

(d) The size of the information files to be retained in marching storage and

(e) The funds available to a library.

In automated library activity, staff and computer share responsibilities for performing work alternatively like a staff member performs the first five processing operations, the computer, the next eight operations and the staff member, the next two operations and so on. Due to sharing of responsibilities the automated activities can be called 'human machine functions'. The computer is merely a tool enabling librarians to do things rapidly, accurately and less expensive than the manual methods. Complete automation without human intervention and control do not exits and are not likely to exit in future.

Q. : Write short notes an following :

– MARC Format

– CCF

– OPAC

Ans.

(1) MARC Format

The introduction of computers in the late 1950s accelerated the use of automated techniques in the Library of Congress (LC). The appointment of King Committee to survey the mechanization in Information Retrieval (IR) in 1958 can be regarded as a cornerstone in the progress towards automation at the LC. The final report of this survey funded by the Council for Library Resources (CLR) was published in 1963. This report envisaged the possibility of automatic the entire bibliographic system of the LC within ten years. Encouraged by this report, the CLR awarded a contract to LC for converting its catalogue to a machine readable form for the purpose of printing bibliographical products by computers. For this LC acquired two big computers, an IBM 1401 with four tape units and an IBM 1403. This study was reported at a conference held in LC in January 1965. In December 1965, LC received a further grant from CLR for the devlopment of a pilot operation to test the feasibility and utility of the distribution of machine readable catalogue data to user libraries. This project was called 'MARC'.

The format for the pilot project which was finalized in April 1966, was termed as MARC-I. The feedback from these libraries led LC to realize the errors in the program and editing, and changes needed in the general format.

The MARC-I which was closely linked to the structure of LC catalogue card needed modification and standardization to meet machine requirements; the format structure of the pilot study which covered only monographs was to be extended to manipulate other forms like serials, periodical literature, etc. and generate related records like name and subject records. Further, the decision to develop an extended character set to cover all the major Roman alphabet language as well as Romanized forms, led to development of MARC-II. The BNB developed a close contact with LC and took part in designing the MARC-II format.

The structure, the content designators and contents are the basic aspects on which the MARC-II format is conceived. The structure, which can be compared to an empty container, provides the basic machine framework of the record. The content designators refer to the means by which elements in the record can be identified, while the content refers to data recorded in the fields. The components of the structure include:

Leader, Record Directory, Variable Field : MARC-II Communication Format Structure has Leader, Record Directory, Variable Fields

Each MARC record contains a leader as the first 24 characters and the leader provides information about the ensuing record such as the total length of the record, the type of record code or the bibliographic level. The type of record code specifies the form of material described in the record as follows:

(a) Language materials, printed e.g., books manuscripts.

(b) Language materials.

(c) Subject authority file.

The bibliographic level code denotes the relationship of the work to another bibliographic entity, for example:

(m) monograph

(s) serial

(a) analytic

(b) collection, etc.

Record Structure/leader (24 characters)	Directory (Variable length)	Data fields (Variable field)	Record Separator (1 character)

Directory

Tag (3 characters) 000 up to 999	Length of data field (4 character) 0000 upto 9999	Starting character position 5 character 00000

Data Elements of Leader	
	Record length (5 character)
	Record status (1character)
	Blank (1 character)
	Bibliographic Level (1 character)
	Indicator length (1 character)
	Sub field identifier (1 character)
	Base address of data (5 character)
	Blank (3 character)
	Length of data field in each directory entry length of implementation defined sections of each directory entry (3 character)
	Blank (1 character)

The second part of the format structure is the record directory. It shows what variable fields are in the record and their location in the record. There is a 12 character record directory for each variable field. It consists of the following:

(i) Tag-three digits identifying a variable field

(ii) Length - four digits

(iii) Starting character position - five digits representing the location of the field in the record.

The existence of a record directory allow one to have variable fields in any order. Updating of the record is facilitated because new fields can be added at the end to the record regardless of what the tags are? The record directory also helps in the retrieval of select fields from the record. An alternative to record directory is to have the tag and length of the field preceding the variable field itself.

Outline of Record Directory Entries : This has following parts.

TAG . Length

Starting character position FIT (Field Terminator)

The last part of the format structure is variable fields.

A variable field consists of the following:

(1) Indicators - two characteristic given additional information about a field.

(2) Sub-field codes-two character

(one alphabetical character) identifying each element in the field.

(3) Data - information pertaining to the field.

(4) Field terminator - special character indicating the end of the field.

The basic framework of the MARC format, consisting of the leader, record directory and variable fields has been adopted as a standard by several organizations.

The MARC format, both by its structure and the content designators, has caused a revolution in the creation of bibliographic database worldwide. The existence of many formats based at least on the principles behind MARC format, proves the impact that MARC has had. The builders of various databases such as INIS, AGRIS and INSPEC have used MARC structure as the basis for the creation of their own communication formats. After record format is decided.

cataloguing entries are prepared according to some standard cataloguing rules such as AACR-2 or adopting ISBD.

(2) CCF or Common Communication Format

Its short name is C.C.F. and it was developed by the UNESCO. The standard of its data and tag at international level was made; for example:

Standard Tag	Standard Name
001	Record Identifier
031	Language and script
100	ISBN
101	ISSN
200	Entries etc.
300	Author etc.
400	Publication

Common Communication format is purely an idea which emphasizes that the information in different computers should be seen in one format. The information should be stored in such a way that it can be transmitted from one place to another in an easy way.

3. On-line Public Access Catalogues (OPACs)

On-line Public Access catalogues are essentially a computer-based replacement of the old card catalogues and its purpose and functions almost remain the same. However, the on-line catalogue is a value-added system, which supersedes the functions of traditional catalogue. It is beyond the capabilities of card catalogue to provide keyword search, Boolean searching and to provide interactive instructions or search facilities to users with possibility of getting outputs in the various formats and information contents they require. In a simple term, it is the machine readable catalogue in place of the card catalogue.

An on-line catalogue reveals to the reader, on the basis of his/her query, whether a book or set of books of his/her interest are, on order, under processing, on the shelf, on loan, sent for binding, misplaced or lost, etc. By developing single or integrated database for all or near all library functions or by way of linking the catalogue, the acquisition system and the circulation system, a library provides bibliographic and status information to the user and staff at one spot, that is on the terminal.

In card catalogue environment, the user moves from physically visible drawer to drawer or from card to card, whereas with on-line catalogues more so in network environment, he or she is faced with a sort of invisible and indiscernible universe.

Retrieval aspects of the OPAC deals with search strategies. The retrieval gives the facility for browsing and searching. The OPACs should allow the users to search by author, title, subject, class number, keywords and boolean search. OPAC is an access tool and resource guide to the library's holdings/collection, which contain bibliographic data in machine readable form. OPACs can also be accessed using Telnet facility over the Network.

The OPACs are the gateways to the bibliographic information in libraries and provide facilities to browse and search and locate the information. If this facility is made available on the Internet, it can be called as Web OPACs. If supported with efficient Document Delivery System, the Web OPACs serve as powerful tool, which will help releasing the resource sharing activity among the libraries.

The libraries use different library application softwares on different platforms with different formats. In this kind of a situation the computers may not be able to communicate in a networked environment to access and retrieve the bibliographic holdings of the libraries. Specially when the OPACs are made accessible over the Internet, there should be standard protocols to enable the computers to establish a connection to send the search request. Z39.50 protocol is a retrieval standard now available. The database server and clients accessing the server should be Z39.50 compliant ignore to connect and communicate and retrieve the information from the Z39.50 compliant server.

Difference between OPAC and Web OPAC

OPAC	*Web OPAC*
The usage is limited to the person in LAN.	The usage is global and any person can access from anywhere.
It is based on the library application software.	HTML files are used with hyperlinks to the subject and other search items.

The operating system environment or the application software, even if they are different the client can comfortably connect and send a search query and get the search result to his/her computer from the remote server.

The on-line catalogues, though, add a layer of functionality by providing various computer supported techniques for searching the data, such as use of system dictionaries, Boolean operators for combining semantic categories or terms regardless of day special citation order, stemming, and truncation etc. At the same time, they also add a layer of complexity to this process, because of the hidden nature of bibliographic records. It has been found that the on-line catalogues are more difficult to use and less serviceable than the card catalogues.

The limitations of on-line catalogues can be removed using traditional facet classification and subject-indexing techniques along with computer supported techniques. For example, the use of (i) facet classification and subject indexing techniques for developing post-coordinating retrieval systems for an on-line catalogue, which use Boolean operators for combining semantic categories or terms regardless of any special citation order, and (ii) truncation of class numbers, particularly provided with the aid of facet classification for retrieving hierarchically different sets of documents.

Insipite of the limitations, OPACs are getting much attraction in the librarian's world for retrieving information regarding collections of the libraries.

4
Networking and Networks

Q. : What is communication ? Discuss the types, methods and mode and media of data transmission.

Or

Write an essay on different types of communication media available for networking.

Ans. Communication in variously defined by different workers. Newsman and Summer has defined Communication as the exchange of facts, ideas, opinions or emotions by two or more persons. Hangman discussed communication as the process of passing information and understanding from one person to another. It is the process of imparting ideas and making one self-understood by other. Chaster Bernard says that, "In any exhaustive theory of organization, communication would occupy a central place because the structure, extensiveness and scope of organizations are almost entirely determined by communication techniques.

In the most fundamental sense, communication involves implicitly the transmission of information from one point of another through a succession of processes. The information being sent from one place to another is also referred as data.

Communication Process

Communication process is a system of exchange of ideas, facts, opinions and manner by which the receiver of the massage shares meaning and understanding with another. There are three basic elements in every communication system; namely the transmitter, the channel and the receiver.

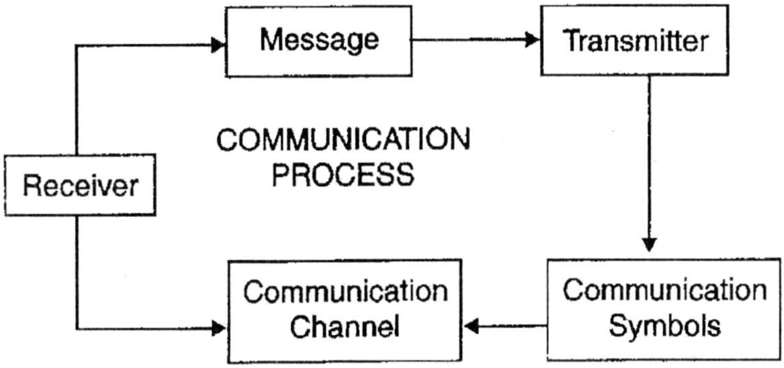

Communication process

The transmitter and the receiver are isolated from each other and it is the channel that connects them together. The transmitter transforms the message signal, produced by source of information into a form suitable for transmission over the channel. As the signal progresses through the channel, noise and other distortion are added to it which corrupt the original signal. The receiver receives this corrupted signal and does the task of converting it back to the original signal and delivers it to the user destination.

Data Transmission

Data communication through computers provides an easy and inexpensive solution to the problem of accessing data at each and every terminal in a multi-user system. Instead of having the same data in each and every computer, thereby utilizing a lot of memory space, all the data can be stored in the memory of one or a few computer systems which can then be accessed by the other terminals linked through direct cables. In the case of geographically dispersed systems data communication provides the most economic way of data sharing with regular updates in the data being accurate in all the terminals at all times.

The data are transmitted through signals. Depending upon the nature of signals there may be Analog transmission and Digital transmission.

(i) Analog Transmission : In analog transmission, there is a continuous up and down pattern. For example, one wave constitutes one cycle, which is measured in the unit called Hertz (cycle per second), the terms cycle and hertz may be used inter-changeable. Thus, it is customary to describe channels as transmitting a certain number of cycles per second (cps).

(ii) Digital Transmission : In digital transmission, wave patterns are translated into discrete bits and are separated by intervals. Bits are the smallest unit of information in data processing. They may be compared to a light-bulb, which is either on or off. When the bulb is on, information is being transmitted; when it is off, there is a blank or interval. In the figure, the upper line of the rectangular wave form represents the bits. The lower line denotes the interval between bits. At this juncture, it must be noted that all electronic transmission can occur in either the analog or the digital mode.

The telephone network, originally intended to carry only the human voice, operates mostly in the analog mode, although all-digital transmission is now available as well. Digital transmission has the advantage of being entirely compatible with computer and terminal originated messages, which also operate in digital mode and of having the capability of transmitting messages more accurately than the analog mode.

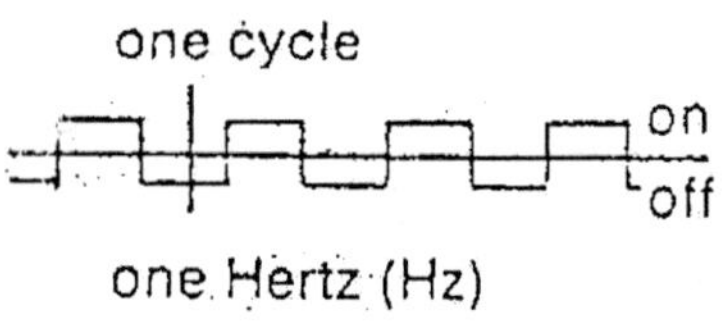

Digital Transmission

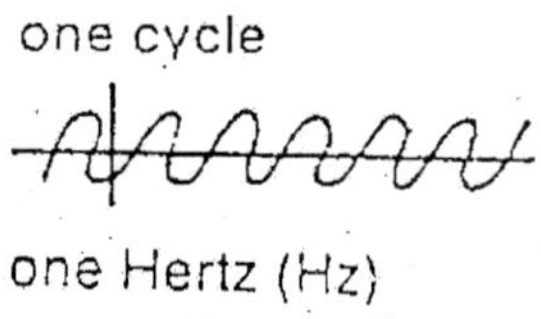

Analog Transmission

Data Transmission

Methods of Transmission

Data can be transmitted in either of the following two ways:

(i) Asynchronous transmission

(ii) Synchronous transmission

(i) Asynchronous transmission: This is the basic method of computer to computer information exchange. It simply means that one character is transmitted at a time.

Start	Character	Parity	Stop

Asynchronous Transmission

Shown above in the figure, is the character along with some bits surrounding it that mark the beginning and the ending of the character. The character here is in the form of bits (0 and 1). This type of transmission is obviously of very low speed since only one character is transmitted at a time.

Because of its nature, asynchronous transmission is often referred to as start stop transmission. Since only one character has to be transmitted at a time. the probability of error occurring in the overall transmission of the data string is very low and almost negligible.

(ii) Synchronous Transmission : Synchronous transmission involves blocking of a group of characters surrounded by synchronization characters. Once the start bit is detected by the receiver it starts receiving the data string (in the form of bits), detected by the receiver it starts receiving the data string (in the form of bits), until the ending bit is encountered. A predetermined number of characters can also be a criterion for the receiver to stop receiving.

Synchronous transmission is obviously much more faster than asynchronous transmission as a number of characters are transmitted in one lot. It ensures efficient utilization of the transmission line. But this type of transmission requires a buffer storage be provided at both ends (receiving as well as transmitting) for assembling and disassembling the data being transmitted. This is also needed for accurately synchronized clock at both ends. It is because of this that the synchronous transmission equipment costs more.

Synch Char.	Char.	Char.	Char.	Parity	Stop

Synchronous Transmission

The above block diagram is depicting the flow of information when synchronously transmitted. The parity is a single byte used for error detection.

Modes of Transmission

A wire pair connecting two telephones is the simplest circuit, allowing communication in both directions. Other channels include coaxial cables, optical fibres, satellites, a light beam, microwaves and others. Whatever the physical medium over or through which message travels, transmission may take place in a number of different modes. They are : Simplex, Half-duplex and Full-duplex.

Simplex : In this type of channel, the message travels in only one direction, that is from point A to point B but not back again.

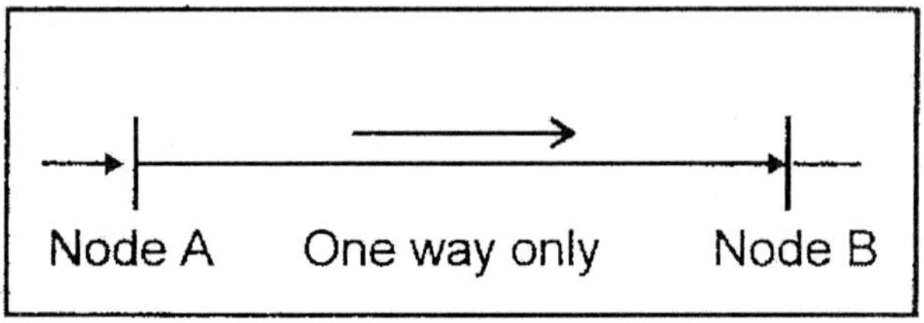

Simplex Mode

Half-Duplex : Here, transmission can take place in either direction, but not at the same time. In other words, message can be transmitted either from A to B or by B to A one at a time.

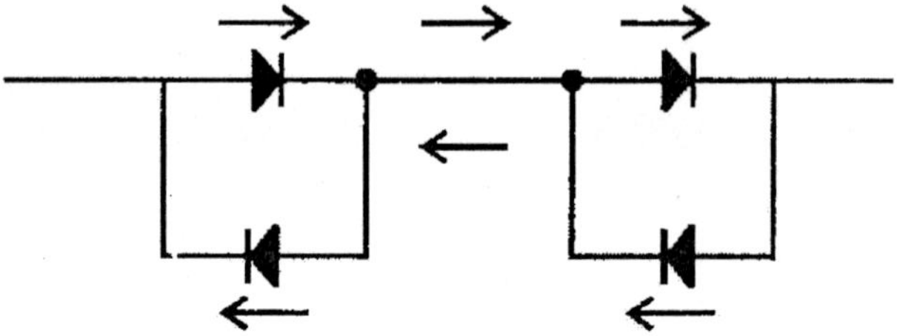

Half Duplex mode

Full-Duplex: In this type of arrangement, message can be transmitted and received over the same channel at the same time.

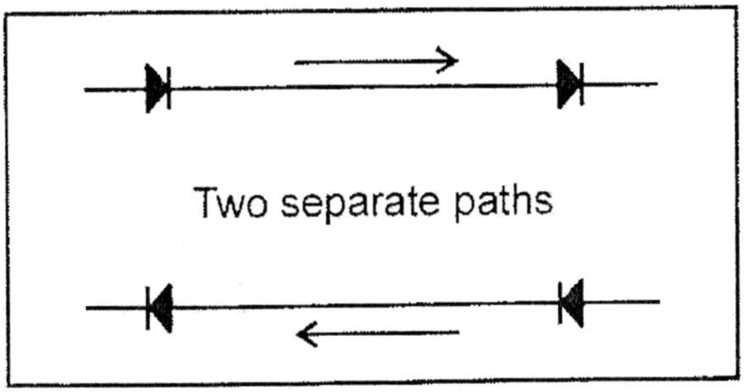

Full Duplex mode

Many libraries and information scientists are familiar with the latter two types because database search terminals must be set to transmit full or half duplex in order to communicate with database vendor's computers.

Transmission Media

Transmission media refers to the medium through which data transmission from the transmitter to the receiver takes place.

The transmission media used in telecommunication networks vary both physically and in their carrying capacity. The commonly used performance measurement of a telecommunication link is its bandwidth. This gives an indication of the range of frequencies which can be transmitted by these channels. The greater the bandwidth, the greater the rate at which data can be transmitted.

The channels or media can be grouped into two main divisions. i.e., line and free space. In the line group, we have two metallic media; twisted pairs and coaxial cables and one optical medium- glass or optical fibres. In the free space category, we have radio propagation which includes broadcast (i.e., TV) and point to point (e.g., microwave signals).

Twisted Pairs : The Twisted Pairs are the copper wire telephone lines. These are of low frequency, and support a limited bandwidth but can also be used for data communication at the lower speeds of 300bps. For higher speed or rates of data transfer, 4-wire leased lines may be used. The problems associate with this kind of transmission are; noise on the line, parity errors and so on. Twisted pairs are used for conventional voice telephone and telex services.

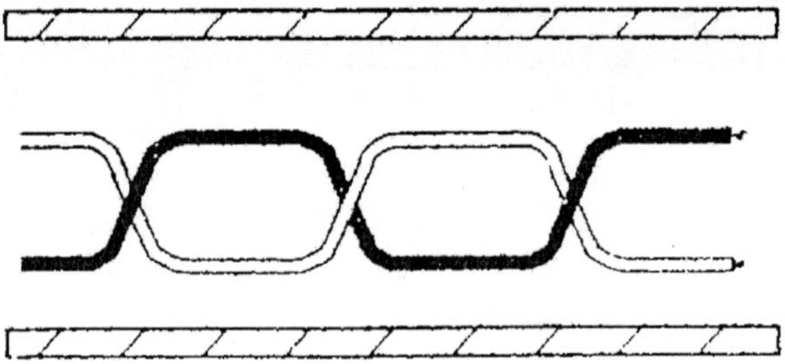

Twisted Pair Cable

Coaxial Cables : These are another metallic transmission media which can transmit data even at very high frequencies and hence they have much higher rate of data transmission than the twisted pair cables. A coaxial cable consists of copper wire surrounded by an insulation and over the insulation a cooper wire mesh is wrapped. This forms an electric shield around the main copper wire and reduces the electromagnetic interference.

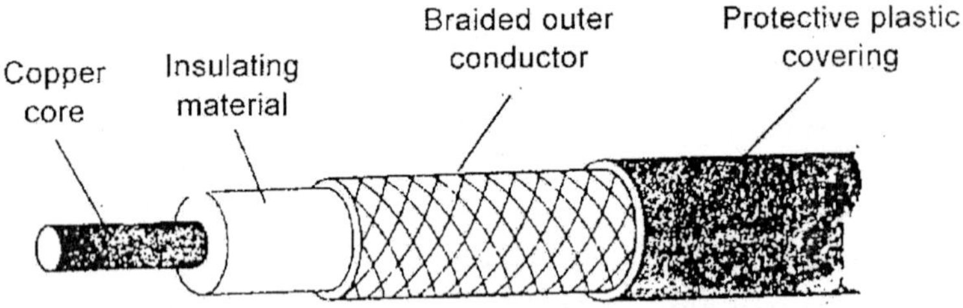

Coaxial Cable

The central cooper wire carries the data while the braided outer conductor prevents the electrical disturbances.

Further, Coaxial cables are of two types:

(i) **Baseband Coaxial Cable :** Baseband Coaxial cables are used for digital data transmission. Therefore, baseband cables are usually employed for LANs.

(ii) **Broadband Coaxial Cable :** Broadband coaxial cables can work at frequencies as high as 450 MHz. Due to this, they can transit many simultaneous signals using different frequencies. The data carried in these cables is essentially analog in nature.

Data transmission through these coaxial cables is very fast and is of the order of gega bits per second. However broadband signals require analog amplifiers after certain distances to strengthen the signal.

Optical Fibres : These are superior over co-axial cables. These cables are very thin tubes made of glass plastic (mostly of silica). The diameter of a glass fiber is very small. Fiber optic transmit light pulses from the light source to the detector. Presence of light indicates a 1 bit and the absence of light indicates a 0 bit. Such a system is known as optical transmission system.

Transmission of data through fiber cables is very fast and most importantly is unaffected by electrical interferences. As compared to a copper telephone line, data transmission through a fiber optic cable is 75,600 times faster.

Fiber optic cables, are much more expensive as compared to copper wires but another advantage they have is that they provide very high bandwidths.

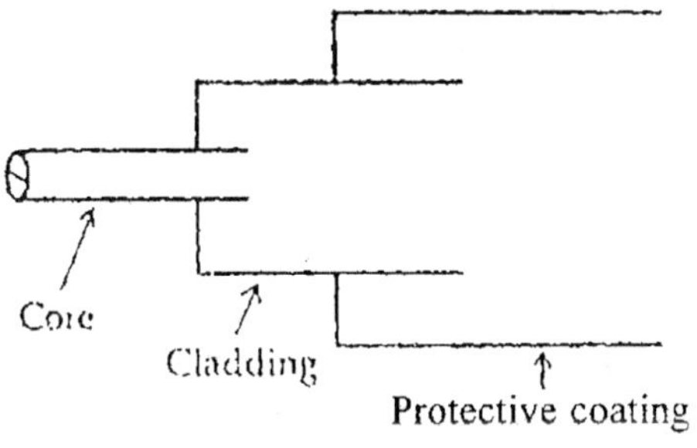

Optical Fibre

But, a repeater is required in fiber optic cables after a certain distances to boost the signal power.

Q. : What do you mean by computer networking? Discuss various types of networking with examples.

Ans. A network consists of two or more computers that are linked in order to share resources such as printers and CD-ROMs, exchange files, or allow electronic communications etc. The computers on a network may be linked through cables, telephone lines, radio waves, satellites or infrared light beams. A typical definition of a data network today would read as : a data network is an interconnected system of computers, peripherals and software over which data, files and messages are sent and received. A more technical definition would be that a devices or nodes that can communicate with each other. The nodes may be computers, terminals, workstations or communication units of various kinds distributed over different locations. They communicate over communication channels that can be leased from common carriers (e.g., telephone companies) or are provided by the owners of the network. These channels may use a variety of transmission media, including optical fibers, coaxial cable, twisted copper pairs, satellite links or digital microwave radio signals.

Over the past decade, modern computer networks have greatly increased in number and geographical area, in the scope of applications supported. A modern network may consist of thousands of computing devices made by various manufactures connected by a variety of transmission media spanning international, and intercontinental boundaries. Though the design, operations and management of such complex systems poses a great challenge.

Network Objectives :

The different types of network that have been evolved to share a set of common objectives. These include the following:

(i) Connectivity to permit different hardware and software products to be connected and communicate with each other;

(ii) Simplicity to permit easy installation and operation of all network components;

(iii) Modularity to enable building a wide variety of network devices from a relatively small set of mass-produced building block;

(iv) Reliability to permit error free transmission by providing appropriate error detection and correction capabilities;

(v) Flexibility to permit the network to evolve as new needs arise or new technologies become available; and

(vi) Diversity of network services that can be easily used and yet isolate users from the technical details of network structure and implementation.

Different types of networks

The networks can be of following types :

1. **Private** - Such networks are usually owned by some corporation or other entity that confines access and use of network services to its staff.

2. **Cooperative-** This refers to networks that are supported and managed by their users. BITNET is an example of this type.

3. **Integrated Services Digital Network (ISDN)-** The development of public data networks for digital communications led to the existence of different networks for different purposes. This resulted in the duplication of networks. To avoid this, interconnection of two or more compatible or incompatible networks to form an internet (network of networks) is attempted. The main aim of ISDN is to build to a public network providing end-to-end digital connectivity which is capable of supporting a range of digital devices and service, both voice and non-voice, on the same basis. This allows users to send and receive data text and image from computer systems as well as offering an enhanced telephone service. This is achieved over a single ISDN connection, so that one network can be used for all applications, providing higher speeds of transmission.

But generally depending upon the distance covered in a network, the networks fall into following types:

- Local Area Network (LAN)
- Metropolitan Area Network (MAN)
- Wide Area Network (WAN)

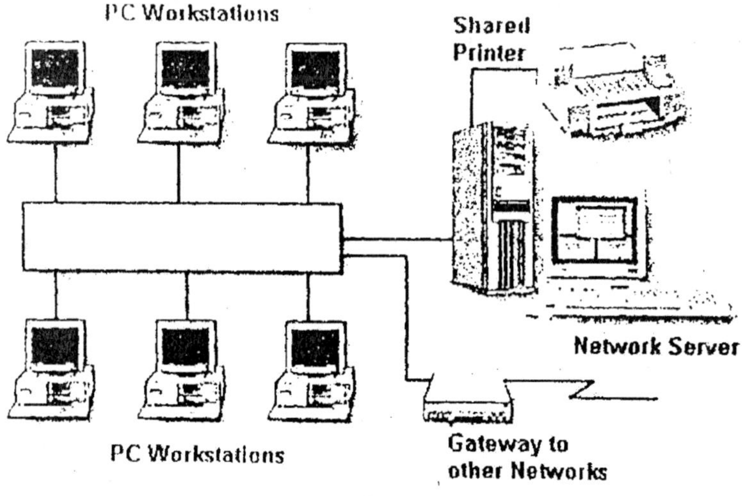

Local area Network (LAN)

1. Local area Networks (LANs)

A Local Area Network connects a large number of different types of equipment, including computer terminals, fax, telex, CD-ROM players. etc. on a single site. The majority of LANs use packet switching technology and offer very high transmission speeds up to one hundred times faster than those available on public networks at present. Most of these are baseband that is they carry only digital computer data, but broadband LANs can carry video and voice signals as well data. The topology of LANs can vary greatly (i.e., linear, star, ring etc.) affecting efficiency, reliability and costs.

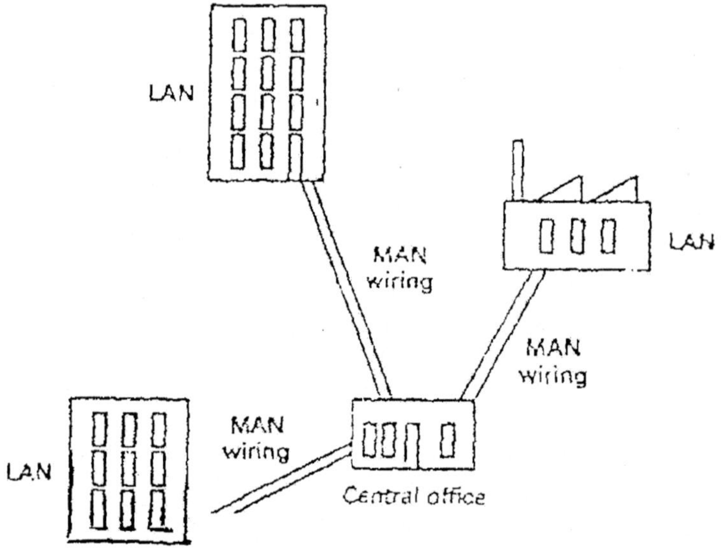

Relationship of LAN and MAN

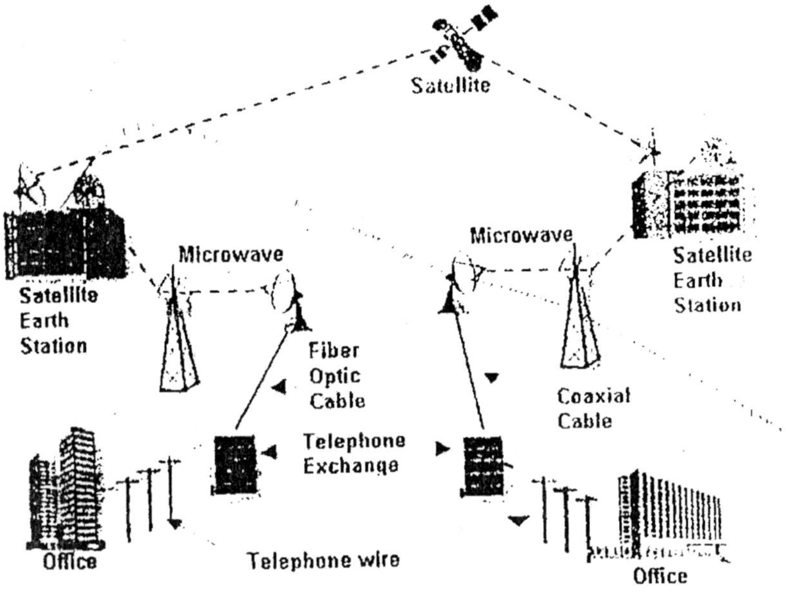

Wide Area Network (WAN)

2. Metropolitan Area Networks

These type of networks cover specific metropolitan area and provide to them all the services. As DELNET covers the network of Delhi Libraries and CALIBNET stands for Calcutta Library networks. The Metropolitan Area Network standards are sponsored by the IEEE, ANSI and the regional Bell Operating Companies. Although 802.6 was designed initially for a LAN to MAN support service, the telephone companies see it as a technology to provide for interconnecting LANs to its central office and even the interconnection of telephone switching facilities.

The MAN standard is organized around a topology and techniques *called dual queue/dual bus* (DQDB). This term means that the topology uses two buses. Each of these buses transmits traffic in one direction only. The implementation for MAN provides for transfer rates from 34 to 150 Mbit/s. The DQDB provides for two types of access. One access is called *pre arbitrated services*, which guarantees a certain amount of "bandwidth" that is useful for isochronous services such as voice and video. The second service is called *queued arbitrated service* and it is based on demand and is designed to accommodate bursted services such as data transmission.

A MAN is designed with two unidirectional buses. Each bus in independent of the other in the transfer of traffic. The topology can be designed as an open configuration or a closed configuration.

3. Wide Area Network (WANs)

These are private networks linking equipment at several different sites and have much in common with conventional large scale data networks.

In configuring a network to communicate information the focus is on minimising costs while maintaining the desired performance standards depend on the nature of the information to be sent. In the case of voice, quality is measured by word intelligibility or articulation index. For video, the Television Allocations Study Organisation has adopted the TASO grades ranging from *excellent to poor* that specify the degree of subjective acceptability of the picture displayed to viewing audiences. For both voice and video, the corresponding quantified measure of quality, signal-to-noise ratio, is used as a technical design parameter. For digital information say from one computer to the other the quality of the transmission is expressed as the number of bit 'errors' a '1' appearing as or vice versa, that occur as a fraction of the total number of bits sent.

Along with performance requirements, it is necessary to choose the channel bandwidth for analog transmission speed of digital signals which is also referred to as data rate or bit rate. These factors partly determine cost. Therefore, depending on whether the transmission is from one point to another, one point several, or several points to a central point, a network is designed. The simplest network might involve just two stations (point to point) link for example to transfer data from one computer to another, or it might be a complicated system where several stations are connected to a local node, several local nodes connected to a central and so on in hierarchical fashion.

Q. : Write a short note of network topology.

Ans. Network of computers is defined as the combination of two or more than two computers for a common purpose or to share their resources.

There are several different ways to organize the computers to form a network. These organizations of the computers in a network are referred to as network topology. These include:

(i) Star Topology
(ii) Ring Topology
(iii) Bus topology
(iv) Mesh Topology
(v) Hierarchical

(i) **Star topology** : In a star topology, server computer is situated at the centre and all workstations are connected directly to it. Here, all the messages are sent through the server. When we send a message from one computer to another, it must go through the server. If the server fails, all network is held up.

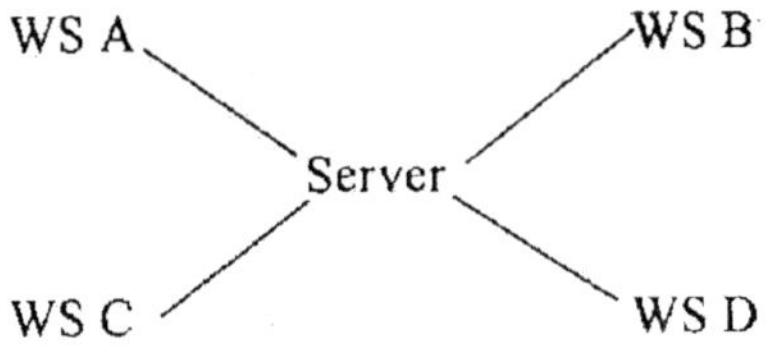

Star Network Topology

(ii) **Ring topology** : In this network topology, the computers and peripheral devices are arranged in a ring like fashion. Here, any computer can communicate with any other computer by sending a signal around the ring. As the message is sent, each computer determines whether it is its message, if not, it is shifted to other computer. It is very similar to bus topology but the only difference is that here a complete loop of the cable is formed.

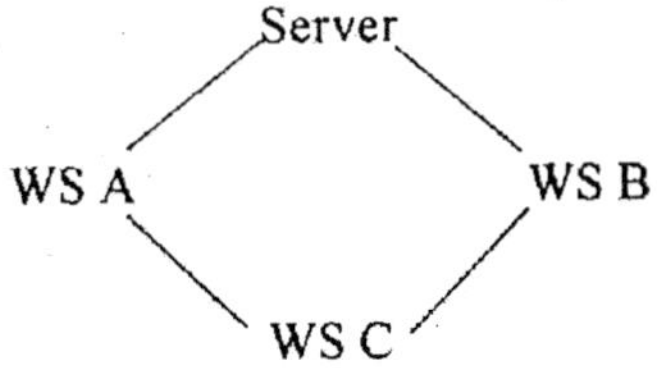

Ring Network Topology

(iii) **Bus topology** : Here, the computers are connected by a cable known as bus and messages are sent along this bus cable. In this topology, the failure of a single computer does not affects the performance of rest of the network.

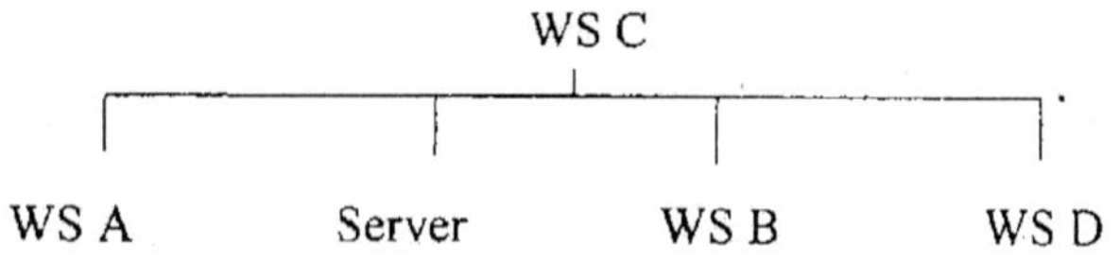

Bus Network Topology

(iv) **Mesh topology** : This topology have multiplicity of paths from server to workstations and permits any two devices to communicate directly within network. It is very dependable because it provides multiple roots into and out of each location. Although this is an expensive one but some users prefer the reliability of this network in comparison of other ones, especially for networks with only a few nodes or workstations.

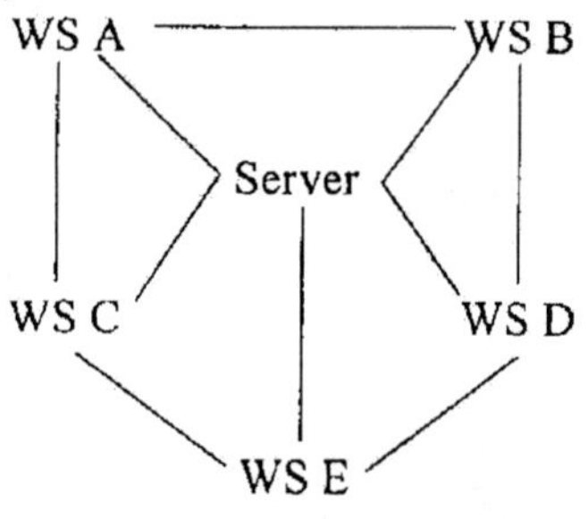

Mesh Network Topology

(v) **Hierarchical topology** : It is also called as tree topology, Here, server computer is situated at the highest order of the hierarchy and workstations are connected in a tree like hierarchical fashion. But the drawback of this topology is that if upper level computer fails to work, the complete network working is held up.

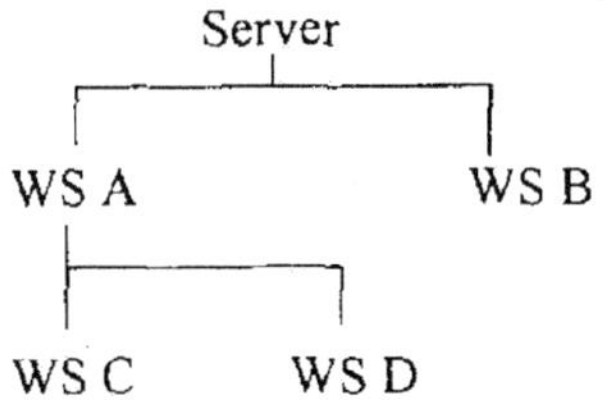

Hierarchical Network Topology

Data transfer using mesh topology is faster than all discussed topologies. Mesh networks are also quite fault resistant. If a particular path fails, data can be routed via alternate paths.

To save on the cost of interconnections and to reduce the complexity of the system, we can make use of the hybrid mesh network. In this type of network some of the main or more frequently used networks are connected to each other like a mesh network.

Q. : What do you mean by library network? Discuss in brief some of the important library networks.

Or

Write short rotes on following –

– CALIBNET

– DELNET

– INFLIBNET

– MALIBNET

Ans. Library Networks usually emphasize, different levels of cooperation among libraries or other participating organizations in the network. According to Library of Congress (LC), the function existing in library network are bibliographic utility and services centres. The main distinction between these functions is based on the product orientation of the bibliographic utility and the distributor orientation of the service centre. Service centres mainly function as access points to provide products and services obtained directly or derived from the bibliographic utilities. In addition to accessing the bibliographic utilities the service centres may also provide to the input data to the storage and retrieval facilities of bibliographic utilities.

The main objective of network among libraries is to serve

cooperation by providing for the sharing and exchange of bibliographic and reference service and text Information.

Range and objectives of Network Services

The range of services provided by many resource sharing networks include storage and retrieval of data such as factual, physical and bibliographic data, document ordering and delivery services, general computer and support of group communication and decision making. The most widely used networks can be described by four major types of services. They are:

- shared cataloguing;
- on-line reference;
- shared circulation;
- interlibrary loan.

Of course, cataloguing networks are by far popular type and are cited as examples of computer applications to library services. Even though library network systems have undergone major development since 1960s and 1970s, the central objectives of networking remain constant. They are:

- to reveal the contents of large number of libraries, especially through accessibility of catalogue databases, using OPAC interfaces;
- to make resources shown in these catalogue databasese available to individual libraries and users when and where they are needed;
- to share the expense and the work involved in creating catalogue databases through the exchange of record and associated activities;

Additional function that might be fulfilled by networks include:

- distribution and publication of electronic journals and other electronic documents;
- end-user access to other databases, such as those available on the online hosts and CD-ROM;
- value-added services such as electronic mail, directory services and file transfer; and
- exchange of bibliographic and authority records usually in MARC format.

Library Networks in USA and UK

The United States has definitely taken a lead in library networking. Among the prominent agencies in this regard, are the Library of Congress, and private agencies like Bibliographic Retrieval Services (BRS), National Medical Library (NLM), Systems Development Corporation (SDC), networks like OCLC (founded in 1971 as Ohio College Library Centre but now known as Online Computer Library Centre), WLN (originally Washington, but now Western Library Network), UTLAS (The University of Toronto Library Automation System) and RLIN (The Research Libraries Information Network) have, layed a major role in the development of library networking.

Of the networks mentioned above, the OCLC (Online Computer Centre) is one of the largest of the bibliographic networks. Though, it is based in the USA, it has world wide library membership including Europe and Far East. OCLC possesses a very large database of MARC format data records and services a large number of libraries for production of their bibliographic databases and for reference and inter-library loan purpose.

Through the late 1980s, OCLC responded to the changing conditions by a gradual opening of access to the existing systems by providing PC-based access rather than by specialized terminal only and by making access links from the Internet research network, which many US academic libraries were beginning to use. This resulted in the establishment of a new X. 25 based network using capacity from the Sprint Commercial value-added network since 1991.

The above development facilitated the introduction of network-to-network links, and the standardization on X.25 rather than proprietary protocols permitted the building of direct links from local area networks thus increasing the connectivity for the user by allowing more flexible mode of connections. Another development that has taken place during this period is that the need for any specialized OCLC hardware, and the development of relevant software to suit it is obviated. Also, the OCLC network service has now taken on a more value added flavour in providing gateway access to other reference services such as the Easynet Information Service, as well as to its own reference network. For instance, the Gateway project allows local network terminals to connect to OCLC ILL and Reference services so that a user may retrieve bibliographic information and locations, and can make a local reservation or request for an inter-library loan.

As is the United States, the first networking activities in the United Kingdom (UK) were associated with centralized cataloguing service. The British National Bibliography (BNB), which is now published by the British Library Bibliographic Services Division has played a very significant role in this respect. A MARC distribution service started in 1969 based on the machine-readable version of the records in BNB, known as the BNB database. At present, it is referred to as BLMARC database, and it includes many other records generated by other sections of the British Library in addition to BNB records. BLAISE (The British Library Automated Information Service) is the major avenue through which BLMARC records can be accessed. Along with these developments, the British Library Document Supply Centre (BLDSC) has established itself as one of the leading document delivery services. The BLDSC also contributed to the Electronic Document Interchange (EDIL) between libraries with partners in other countries. In UK, there are also a number of library networks.

Some of the major ones are: the BLCMP (formerly known as the Birmingham Libraries Cooperative machanisation Project) is a cooperative venture which provides a range of services that are utilized by a large number of libraries. The BLCMP maintains extensive MARC database. The LASER (The London and South Eastern Region) is another network effort with an emphasis on resource sharing and interlending apart from cataloguing service. A significant development in LASER in recent years is the starting of the project Electronic Access to Resources in Libraries (EARL) in the year 1995. This project is intended to develop the role of public libraries in providing library and information services over the network. More than 50% of public libraries are its members. EARL's contributions include EARL Web, which is a network of public library information services, and a consortium purchase deal to OCLC's First Search Service.

JANET (the Joint Academic Network) is another important functioning network in U.K. It is not a library network, but a telecommunications network that provides communication links between users of computing facilities in more than 100 universities, research establishments and other institutions. JANET has been widely used by libraries for mutual access to library OPACs and for file transfer and electronic mail. It provides gateway approaches to other data networks and Internet.

Another important networking service is BIDS offered by the UK office for Library Networking with funding from British Library. BIDS has played a very important role in making electronic database available at competitive rates within UK academic community.

Library and Information Networks in India

India is spending more than Rs. 5000/- million a year on procuring new library resources and of that around Rs. 2000/- million is spent on the acquisition of overseas journals. The annual increase in price of these resources means that even financially sound organizations experience difficulties in meeting their cost. Also, the increase in information generation at an estimated rate of 13% per annum has made the task of collection, organization and retrieval of information very difficult. These two main factors have influenced libraries and information centers to automate their services and share resources through networking.

Today networking is one of the most effective ways of sharing the resources, which are always scarce to meet the information needs of the users. The growth can be traced to some of the policies that Government of India pursued during the last decade. For instance, the Technology Policy Statement (1983) realized the importance of Scientific and Technical Information (STI) and rightly emphasized the need for a technology information base. Also, in 1984, the Planning Commission Constituted a Working Group under the chairmanship of Dr. N. Seshagiri which recommended to the Government the need for the modernization of library services and informatics during the 7th plan period (1985 to 1990). In the same report, the Working Group recommended the interlinking of library systems in the country using modern information technology. The National Library and Information Policy document submitted in 1988 contained a recommendation to the effect that modern information technology must be used at national level to improve the library and information services in the country and make them more purposive and user-oriented. It is NISSAT (National Information system for Science and Technology) which took initiative for the establishment of CALIBNET in Calcutta and supported the formation of DELNET in 1988 and PUNET in Pune in 1992, ADINET in Ahemdabad in 1993, and BONET in Mumbai in 1994. In another effort INSDOC (Indian Nation Scientific Documentation Centre) Delhi took initiative and supported the formation of MALIBNET in Chennai in 1998. BALNET in Bangalore was registered as a society in 1997. The UGC did not lag behind in networking effort either. It established INFLIBNET in 1988 itself which is a network of University and College Libraries and became operational in 1991.

Moreover, in December 2003 a major network UGC-INFONET has already been launched to provide e-access of journals and data bases throughout all universities in India.

It is important to mention here the Report of the Planning Commission on Libraries and Informatics for the Ninth Five Year Plan (1997-2002) which prepared under the chairmanship of Shri B.P. Singh, the then Secretary, Department of Culture. This document is a significant one in the sense that it is comprehensive and contains recommendations of far reaching consequence, if implemented fully. It has a large number of recommendations on the modernization as well networking of libraries including public libraries.

Non-Bibliographic Data Networks in India

Some of the significant data communication networks functioning in the country are :

The National Informatics Center (NIC) was established in 1975. One of its objectives was build into intra-city and inter-city computer networks for interconnecting various ministries/departments of the central government and autonomous organizations for a distributed governmental information system. To fulfill this objective, the NIC established NICNET in 1977. It links regional nodes at Delhi, Pune, Bhuwaneswar and Hyderabad and 32 nodes at state and union territory levels and 439 nodes at district headquarters. NICNET is based on spread spectrum multiple access technique and uses C-2000 series of micro-earth stations. NICNET has created a number of databases and networking. Many information systems have been designed and established by NIC for the purposes of providing administrative information support for the efficient functioning and management of the central government. All these databases can be accessed through NICNET. It also provides the facility for the transmission of bibliographic data.

Another effort in this direction is the establishment of INDONET, which has an integrated information management and distributed data processing facility. It is a commercial network with nodes at Kolkata Mumbai and Madras (Chennai). It is connected to cities like Ahmedabad, Bangalore, Delhi and Pune through MUXs/cluster controllers. INDONET uses IBM's System Network Architecture (SNA). It is planned as a geographically dispersed computer network linking scattered organizations in the country.

VIKRAM is yet another public data network established by the Department of Telecommunications. It is a packet switched data network having its management centre at Delhi and switching nodes at Bombay (Mumbai), Callcutta (Kolkata), Madras (Chennai), Bangalore, Hyderabad, Ahmedabad and Pune with 12 remote access points.

The Department of Electronics established ERNET mail during the Seventh Plan (1986-1991) to provide academic and research institutions with electronic mail facilities. It is used by many academic and research institutions.

There are other similar efforts in this direction but the Gateway Packet Switching System (GPSS) is one of the significant moves. The GPSS established Packed Assembler-Dissemblers (PADs) in Delhi, Madras (Chennai), Bangalore, Hyderabad and Pune. Networks like NICNET, INDONET and VIKRAM are connected to this gateway.

IMPORTANT LIBRARY NETWORKS OF INDIA

Some of the important library networks working in India are briefly discussed below:

1. INFLIBNET (Information and Library Network)

The University Grants Commission (UGC) in its attempt to establish networking has taken the initiative and decided to develop a network of academic libraries to mange effectively and administer the resources of these libraries and provide efficient library services to a large number of users, using modern computer and communications technologies. As a consequence of UGC's efforts INFLIBNET, a network of university and college libraries in India was established in 1988, which became functional in 1991.

UGC had drafted a new Memorandum of Association and Rules and registered the INFLIBNET Society in the year 1996. The objectives included in this Memorandum of Association are different from those recommended in the working Group Report of 1988. However, it may be noted here that the INFLIBNET Review Committee under the chairmanship of Dr. S. Venkateswaran in its report, submitted in 1996, also recommended revision of the objectives for INFLIBNET.

The main objectives INFLIBNET are :

- To evolve a national network of libraries and information centres in the country and to improve information handling capability;
- To provide reliable access to document collection through online union catalogue;
- To provide better access to bibliographic information sources with citation and abstracts through online accessing of international databases held by international information networks and centres;
- To provide document services by establishing resource centres around libraries having a rich collection of documents;
- To promote information resource utilization through shared cataloguing inter-library loan service;
- To computerise operations of libraries and information centres in the country following a uniform standard;
- To facilitate communication among scientists, engineers, researchers, social-scientists, academics, faculties, and students through electronic-mail;
- To enable users regardless of location and distance to access information;
- To create online information service and;
- To encourage cooperation among libraries.

Activities

INFLIBNET is also engaged in the manpower development activity by undertaking some short term training programmes and workshops. The network has also develop a standarized software, which in known as SOUL. Much is expected of this network. Some of the databases develop in INFLIBNET are mentioned below:

(i) **Books Database :** Union Database of books represents the collection held by the participating libraries under INFLIBNET programme. Database covers monographs, reference books, conference proceedings, and textbooks etc., which are normally classified by the universities under book collection. Currently, this database has few lakh of records and is continuously growing. It provides minimum bibliographic information contributed by the universities about each book along with the library name. To search this database, the following access points can be used: Title, Author, Publisher, Keywords, and ISBN No.

(ii) **Serial Holding Database :** This union database of serial holding covers the bibliographic information of serials available in more then 150 University/Institute libraries. Serials, learned journals, periodicals classified under the serial collection by the universities are coverd in this database. Minimum bibliographic information along with holdings details and university name is provided for each record.

(iii) **Secondary Serial Database :** Union database of Secondary Serials is yet another new database started from 1999. This database covers some unique titles subscribed by more than 150 universities/institute libraries. This database provides the listing of titles with brief bibliographic information along with the library name. The titles treated as Secondary Serial viz, abstracting, indexing etc. are coverd here. Some of the titles available in CD-ROM or Diskette form are also covered in this Database. To search this database one may use the access points, like Title, ISSN, Frequency, Publisher, Place of Publisher, Keywords, Library. etc. to retrieve the information.

(iv) **Current Serials Database :** Union database of current serials is one of the major databases developed by INFLIBNET covering 11,892 unique titles subscribed by more than 197 universities/ institute libraries. This database provides the listing of titles with brief bibliographic information along with the library name.

2. CALIBNET (Calcutta Library Network)

The formation of Calcutta Library Network (CALIBNET) is the result of the efforts made by NISSAT (National Information System for Science, and Technology). The Department of Scientific and Industrial Research initiated action for this purpose. Accordingly a feasibility study report for networking about 40 libraries in Calcutta was prepared by the CMC Limited. As per the details contained in the report, an amount Rs. 233.8 lakhs was to be spent during the two phases of its implementation. The software required for this purpose was to be developed by CMC Limited based on INGRES 5.2 for CALIBNET with the financial support of NISSAT. The package named MAITRAYEE was developed and handed over to CALIBNET. It is understood that no database has been created using MAITRAYEE package in machine-readable form. It appears that no automation activity has yet been commenced utilising MAITRAYEE by any of the libraries, which were expected to be the participation members of CALIBNET. It is stated that CALIBNET is presently playing the role of a centre for CD-ROM databases which are acquired from outside sources.

Libraries can access these CDs. The basic purpose of the library network is to share the resources available in participating libraries. However, no resource sharing is done, as there is no union catalogues prepared. This activity is however, in progress.

Activities

Some of the major activities of CALIBNET are as below:

(i) **Union List of Current Serials held in Kolkata Libraries :** A union list of current serials held in Kolkata libraries has been prepared. Search can be made through Title, and by the host library.

(ii) **ASJI Database :** A union list of journals subscribed by Asiatic Society has been prepared. The search can be made by Title, Publication Year etc. The database contains indices to the Serialized Publications of the Asiatic Society.

(iii) **Conference Proceedings :** A database of conference proceedings of the seminars/conferences held by the CALIBNET is prepared. The search can be made through Title, Venue and Year of the conference.

(iv) **Union Catalogue of Social Science Serials** : This contains holdings of select management and development libraries in India, and one each in Bangladesh, Pakistan, Sri Lanka and Bhutan. It is developed in continuation of the database built under AMDISA Project. Search can be made by Title and Host Library Name.

3. DELNET

The DELNET is established in 1988 by India International Centre with the initial financial support of NISSAT and later official registered as a society in June 1992. Its main objectives are:

(i) to promote sharing of resources among the libraries by developing a network of libraries, by collecting, storing and dissemination information and by offering computerized services to the users;

(ii) to offer guidance to the member libraries on cataloguing, database services, circulation, acquisition, serials control, online services, selection of hardware and software, etc.;

(iii) to coordinate efforts for suitable collection development and reduce unnecessary duplication wherever possible;

(iv) to establish a referral centre, to monitor and/or facilitate catalogue search and maintain a central online union catalogue of books, serials, and non-book materials of all the participating libraries;

(v) to facilitate and promote delivery of documents manually and mechanically;

(vi) to develop specialist bibliographic database of books, serials and non-book materials;

(vii) to develop database of projects, specialists and institutions;

(viii) to possess and maintain electronic and mechanical equipment for fast communication of information and delivery of electronic mail;

(ix) to coordinate with other regional, national and international networks for exchange of information and documents; and

(x) to undertake, facilitate and provide for the publication of newsletters and/or journals devoted to networking and sharing of resources.

Activities

DELNET offers to its member libraries the undermentioned services:

(i) Online and off-line access to its databases;

(ii) Ill online: Inter-Library loan requests are entertained online for books and other documents;

(iii) INTERNET and E-mail Services: E-mail and Internet connectivity being provided by NIC to DELNET is being extended to all the member libraries at reduced rates. ERNET E-mail is also being provided;

(iv) DELNET-LISTSERV (INTERNET mailing list): Online information on IFLA, Library and information science jobs, happendings and Medical Clippings;

(v) Online information about forthcoming and new titles from publishers, book reviews, and current contents from INTERNET:

(vi) DELNET conducts training programmes and workshops, seminars and lectures;

(vii) Offers retro-conversion facilities to member libraries through equalised agencies; and

(viii) DELNET had created a Web-page on INTERNET HYPERLINK http://www.nic.in/delnet. In addition to the above services, DELNET main objective is to promote sharing to resources among the libraries located in Delhi and outside Delhi. It is the first operational library network in India and has developed databases mentioned below;

(i) Union Catalogue of Books in CCF : DELNET maintains an online union catalogue of books available in its member-libraries. This union catalogue is continuously updated and is growing in size. The information can be retrieved by author, title, subject, conference, series, etc. The request for inter-library loan can also be placed through the online system.

(ii) Union Catalogue of Books in MARC Format : MARC is an internationally used format for machine-readable bibliographic records. DELNET has introduced CCF for the creating of records in

MARC format. It has presently 44, 132 records. DELNET has separately created a union catalogue of books for MARC records.

(iii) Union List of Current Periodicals : DELNET has created union list of current periodicals in science and technology, social sciences and humanities. This databases is available online to DELNET users. It now lists 21,331 periodicals and is regularly updated and new titles are added annually.

(iv) Union Catalogue of Periodicals : DELNET maintain a union catalogue of periodical which contains full holdings data of the libraries. At present the databases contains 19,289 records.

(v) Databases of Periodical : The database has details of articles, which can be searched under the title, author. There are approximately 5.0 lakh records.

(vi) CD-ROM Databases : A bibliographic database of CD-ROMs available with the member-libraries has been started recently and is available online. There are about 2000 records.

(vii) Union list of Video Recordings : This is a database of videocassettes available in DELNET member libraries and has about 4000 listings.

(viii) Union List of Sound Recordings : This union list consists of 748 audio-cassette records available in member-libraries.

(ix) Union List of Newspapers : This database lists newspapers being subscribed by Delhi Libraries. It contains information about the newspapers including title, name of the editor, published from e-Mail address and also the web address of the INTERNET edition, if available. There are 70 records in this database.

(x) Union List of Serials of Management Libraries : DELNET has recently constituted as Sub-Committee for rationalizing the periodicals in the Management Sector Libraries in and around Delhi. It contains nearly 800 serials.

(xi) Union Catalogue of Hindi Books : The database contains nearly 3000 records in Hindi and can be retrieved thorough the GIST compatible system.

(xii) Multilingual Books Sample Database : DELNET has also prepared a sample database of language publications of various I-

and some foreign languages using GIST technology. This acts as a guideline for member-libraries wishing to create databases other than in English.

(xiii) Urdu Manuscripts Databases : DELNET has created an Urdu manuscripts database, which is available, online to member-libraries and lists 210 manuscripts. It contains a descriptive bibliography on a variety of subjects such as animal husbandry, astronomy, teaching techniques, ethics, Arabian history, letter writing, literary criticism. Islamic sects, Jehad, theology, sports, etc. The maximum number of entries are on poetry, fiction and Islam.

(xiv) Database of Thesis and Dissertations : DELNET has recently started the database on theses and dissertations available in various member-libraries. This database is steadily growing in size and now has over 41420 records.

(xv) Serial Database of Petroleum and Natural Gas : A serials database on the current periodicals available in Petroleum Natural Gas libraries in India has been started recently and is available online. It has nearly 1000 records.

4. MALIBNET

To face the challenges of meeting the growing information demands of the user community and obviating the problems of resource crunch in libraries, MALIBNET-a registered society was formed in 1993, through an MOU. INSDOC has been entrusted the responsibility of setting up and provides technical support for operating the network.

Presently nearly 50 libraries in Madras are contributing actively to the creation of various databases on MALIBNET. With the help of communication links and sophisticated information technology, the resources of the member libraries are shared and made available to the users.

The major achievements of MALIBNET are :

(i) **Directory of Databases of Current Serials :** It contains information of 5200 serials currently subscribed by 50 libraries in Madras (Chennai). It covers journals of basic sciences, applied science and technology, medicinal science and life science disciplines which is available online and on diskette and can be searched by title, subject and by library options.

(ii) **Contents Database :** It holds article index of nearly 500 journals online, and is Searchable through author, title and keyword options.

(iii) **Specialized Database for Automotive Industries :** It covers valuable National and International journals in the field. It has currently around 10000 records and is updated regularly. Search options are available-by journal, keyword and author.

Status of some important library networks in India

Name	Year of Starting	Promoting Agency	Whether Registered as Society	Database Development
ADINET	1993	INLIBNET, NISSAT	Yes	1. Library holdings database in progress of 2. Current periodicals of member libraries
BALNET, Bangalore	1995	NISSAT	Yes	1. Work is yet to be started
BONET, Mumbai	1994	NCST, NISSAT	No	1. Online Union Catalogue 2. Database of content of Indian Periodicals
CALIBNET, Kolkata	1992	NISSAT	Yes	1. Work is under progress
DELNET, Delhi	1990	NIC & NISSAT	Yes	1. Union catalogue of book & journals 2. Database of journal articles 3. CD-ROM databases 4. Union list of sound/ recordings 5. Urdu manuscript database 6. Database of theses dissertations
INFLIBNET Ahemdabad	1991	UGC	Yes	1. Union Catalogue of 50000 records 2. Database of periodical 3. Contents with abstract services
MALIBNET, Chennai	1993	NISCAIR	Yes	1. Current Serials Database 2. Journals' Contents

Name	Year of Starting	Promoting Agency	Whether Registered as Society	Database Development
				Database 3. Automotive Engineering Database
MYLIBNET, Mysore	1994	Mysore Library Consortium	Yes	1. Vidhyanidhi 2. Serials catalogue
PUNENET, Pune	1992	UOP/CDAC/ NCL	Yes	1. Union catalogue of books periodicals.

5. PUNENET

Pune Net is a joint programme of the university of Pune, Centre for Development of Advanced Computing and the National Chemical Laboratory. The project is funded by NISSAT. Its objective of is to open the door to the information available in the libraries and other resource centres in Pune. PUNENET Maintains centralized book, periodicals and professional databases of the participating libraries. The other objective is to help increasing cooperation among the participating libraries holdings and coordinates their activities, so as to serve the user community effectively.

At present PUNENET hosts the databases mentioned below. These databases are updated annually. Users can search these databases online using its website.

(i) **Database of Books:** The database contains 1,08,835 records from 20 participants libraries of PUNENET. A user can conduct simple or Boolean search to locate the desired item.

(ii) **Union Catalogue of Periodicals :** This database contains 6425 records pertaining to various libraries in the Pune city. Currently data from 60 libraries are available online.

6. BONET

The Bombay Library Network (BONET) sponsored by the NISSAT, aims at promoting cooperation among libraries in Mumbai. The National Centre for Software Technology (NCST), one of the eight participating institutions of ERNET functions as the central node of BONET. The NCST has made available on HP* @ minicomputer (NOVA) with one gadgety disk and a RDBMS software for inter library activities. The BONET will use local dial-up PSTN communication facilities for linking the libraries, the member libraries are however urged to use lease lines to fully benefit from the online services. The BONET will also offer the training related to computerization and networking to the participating libraries.

7. ADINET

ADINET is the network of member libraries of Ahmedabad, It was registered as a society in Oct 1994 and is sponsored by the National Information System for Science and Technology (NISSAT), Department of Scientific and Industrial Research Goverment of India. ADINET aims at promoting resource sharing and dissemination of information among member libraries by networking and creating a centralized union catalogue of their holdings.

8. MYLIBNET

The NISSAT, Department of Scientific and Industrial Research (DSIR) took up initiation for the design and development of library networks in India in 1985 in order to share the resources available in the libraries in various parts of the country. The Mysore Library Network was set up during May 1995 in the city of Mysore under the financial assistance from NISSAT. It has developed the following databases:

(i) **Vidyanidhi :** Vidyanidhi is a Digital Library Interactive currently underway at the Department of Library and Information, University of Mysore, India. This initiative is sponsored by NISSAT, DSIR, Government of India. The full texts of thesis are available online submitted in Indian universities. Full text search allows user to search theses by author, keyword, language and university etc.

(ii) **Serials Catalogue :** A union catalogue of S & T serials in Mysore City Libraries with the financial assistance from NISSAT was completed. The catalogue is available online. Search can be made by the title/keyword in the title of the journal. For institutions, a drop-down list it is given from which it can be selected.

Concluding, it can be seen except DELNET and INFLIBNET, most of the other library networks have yet to develop databases of library holdings in a significant way. Even these two networks have to go a long way, to cover in their databases, the entire holdings of all the participating libraries. Unless this is achieved, the networks would not be able to achieve significant resource sharing as well as rationalization in library acquisitions. Most of the networks are, however, making efforts towards this end by conducting training programmes for the staff of the participating libraries in data capturing, database development and automation of library activities and services.

5

Miscellaneous

Q. : What is Internet? Briefly describe it and discuss impact of Internet on library services.

Ans. The roots of the Internet lie in a project called the ARPANET, which was sponsored by the United States Department of Defence, Advanced Research Projects Agency (ARPA). The department of defence was interested in building a network that could maintain itself under adverse conditions.

The project was started in 1968 and soon evolved into a more general goal of developing techniques to build a large-scale network. ARPANET continued for years and was gradually phased out after having been officially declared completed. By then, the technology to connect computers reliably and economically had been developed and today the ARPANET's spiritual descendents form the global backbone of what we call, INTERNET, is simply defined as network of networks. It consists of a large number of linked computer networks forming a global network. This is largely open and free, allowing users to communicate with each other for work and recreational purposes, and for corporate and personal reasons. Because the Internet is so vast and is without regulation or hierarchy, the network is a treasure-trove of information from many sources. Resources are available in all subjects; mailing is possible for all the participants; documents can be forwarded and delivered across the world and directories and journals abound. The developments such as the World Wide Web (WWW) combine friendliness of user interface with enormously powerful information retrieval capability. Electronic mail is one of the most important services offered through the Internet, with each person having a personal mail address, enabling them to link up to another user anywhere in the world and communicate within seconds. In other words, it is easier to view the Internet in two related but distinct parts; they are the communications network, which is the immence web of interconnected local and wide area networks, telephone lines, cables, fibre-optics and satellite links which provide the medium for the transfer of information around the Internet, and the computers and computing sites which actually hold and process the data which are available to be transmitted across the network.

To go for Internet, basically following requirements are needed.

* A *computer* with the right software.
* The use of a *telephone line* or cable with a suitable socket.
* A *modem* to connect the computer to the telephone line.
* An account with an *Internet Service provider (ISP).*

Any of the PC models available today e.g., Intel, Celron, Intel PII, Intel PIII, Intel PIV, AMD K6, CYRIX MII, etc., can be used. The CPU of 350 MHz and above gives a good performance. Atleast 64-Mb RAM has good navigation on the net. The AGP card should have at least 4Mb RAM. This helps in watching the graphics/moves on the Internet effectively. As far as the software part is concerned, there are two sets of software that are needed.

The first is the basic *Internet access software*, which is system software to set up and control the connection to your computer's operating system to Internet.

Internet access software must be successfully installed and running before you can use the second sort software, *Internet application software*, such as Web Browsers, email or newsreaders. Internet access software has two key components:

A *dialer* to instruct the modem to dial the right phone number, and to identify your machine to the access provider's system for access to the network.

TCP/IP network software to allow programs on your computer to communicate properly over the Internet once a connection has been set up.

A modem is a device or program that enables a computer to transmit data over telephone lines. Computer information is stored digitally, whereas information transmitted over telephone lines is transmitted in the form of analog waves. A modem converts between these two forms.

There are two types of modems –

(1) **Acoustic Coupler Modem :** These modems do not require a direct connection to the computer. Instead the telephone headset is inserted in to the modem's rubber cups.

(2) **Direct Connect Modem :** A direct connect modem makes a direct connection between the computer and the telephone line. Direct connect modems are again of two types-

(a) **External direct connect modems :** External direct modems are externally connected to the computer and usually have a separate power supply. The external modem is also sometimes referred to as the "intelligent modem" because of its ability to automatically dial, redial and disconnect.

(b) **Internal direct connect modems:** An internal direct connect modem is a printed circuit board which is plugged into one of the slots provided in the computers motherboard.

Direct connect modems are superior to acoustic couplers for almost every telecomputing application. They are usually easier to use, less expensive and more reliable.

Internet Service Provider is a company that provides access to the Internet. For a monthly fee, the service provider gives you a software package, username, password and access phone number. Equipped with a modem, you can then log on to the Internet and browse the World Wide Web and USENET and send and receive e-mail.

In addition to serving individuals, ISP also serve large companies, providing a direct connection from the company's networks to the Internet. ISPs themselves are connected to one another through *Network Access Points (NAPs).*

Famous ISP's in India are –VSNL (Videsh Sancher Nigam Ltd.), Mantra, and Satyam.

Dial-up Networking (DUN) is Microsoft's dialer software, responsible for making, connections to remote systems. The DUN software consists of a number of components, which together handle your end of an Internet connection. The other speed lines are :

ISDN (Integrated Service Digital Network) is the only higher-speed system. ISDN works over ordinary telephone cable, and call charges are the same, but the start-up costs can be high.

ADSL is a new system that will offer several times the speed of basic ISDN, but still be capable of using existing telephone exchange lines, so minimizing the cost.

Cable Modem is an extra-cost option on some Cable TV systems. It promises high speed and low call costs, but is available only in certain cabled cities.

Getting on-Line

For getting on-line, following steps are proceeded –

(i) the first job is to install a network protocol -- the software that allows a computer to communicate with other on Internet. This is done through the Network Icon in the control panel. The steps to be followed are –

- Open the Control panel and run the Network Properties.
- Click the Add Button.
- At the next panel, select Protocol and Click ADD.
- Select Microsoft then TCP/IP and click OK.

Once, this has been installed, the computer – will be restarted.

(ii) the second step is the making of the connection. This needs the following steps –

- Open the Start Menu and select Programs – Accessories – Dial-Up Networking or My Computer and double-click Dial-up-Networking.
- When the Dial-up Networking folder opens, click Make new Connection. This runs a Wizard to collect the name and phone number for the provider, and creates an icon for the new connection.
- Click on your new connection to start it up. The connect dialog box will open.
- Type in your user name and password.
- It the set-up is confirmed, then you can click on the explorer or navigator and can access the Internet.

Internet Services

There are available a number of services on Internet but following two are most wide by used and appreciated ones –

(i) Email : The first killer application on the Internet was *e-mail*. This was the most immediately visible benefit of connecting early computer networks together. It allowed academic researchers to exchange electronic messages and distribute information almost instantly, even when they were in establishments many miles apart and used different local systems.

The advantages of e-mail were not lost on business users, particularly those already familiar with computers and e-mail fuelled the spread of the Internet to general office use.

(ii) **The World Wide Web** : The other killer application, and the one that really launched the internet onto the public stage, is the *World Wide Web.* The Web provides a framework for organizing and presenting almost any kind of written, graphical or audio-visual information from anywhere in the world.

Besides the Internet can also :

- transfer computer files and software electronically from anywhere in the transfer computer files and software electronically from anywhere in the world.
- Carry electronic discussion services.
- Provide access to information services.
- Carry digital sound and images.
- Provide remote control of distant computers.

Impact of the Internet on Libraries

While the internet revolution is leading to big changes for librarians all over the world, it is still in its infant stage in the Indian libraries. Though, there are a very few technocrats who have just jumped on the bandwagon to make everything computerized and networked yet a large number of librarians have not kept pace with the technology. They are silent spectator of whatever happens and want someone else to do for them. It should be realised that Internet will help libraries in following areas:

(a) By designing clearly organised, easily accessible and well published web sites, the librarians can extend the traditional librarianship to the use of information technology and series a leadership role in both fields.

(b) The libraries can initiate Bulletin Board Service which gives complete information regarding services, products, and various events organized by them.

(c) Ready reference service can be provided with greater speed and in much shorter time.

(d) Books and journals can be ordered online, technical processing of the documents too can be done without much efforts.

(e) E-mail services can be used for delivering information to the users and communicating with the fellow information professionals.

(f) E-SDI services can be used for delivering information professionals.

(g) Access to various databases and OPAC of other libraries located in remote areas can be provided.

Role of Internet in Discharging Library Functions

Internet is playing an important role in discharging the functions of libraries. It is changing the ways of organizing, managing and disseminating the information. Today all sorts of library services from membership registration to document delivery can be offered through the Internet. Some of the important library services that can be offered through the Internet are as follows:

(i) Acquisition of Documents : Internet has made simple and speedy purchase of information sources/documents like books, journals and electronic publications. A number of commercial databases are available for librarians to exploit viz, the *CAB abstracts*, *Agricold, Medline, Agris, Biological Abstracts, Compendex*, etc. of Dialog and BRS Information Technology.

Most of the publishers and booksellers have their web sites on the Internet and place their regular catalogues and leaflets of new publications. Some of the publishers of primary journals like American Chemical Society, IEEE (USA), Elsevier Science Publishers, are providing their journals online. The IDRC, Canada is providing books on research and development that can be ordered online through the URL http://www.idrc.ca/bookhque. It also publishes its best reports online which are also available at web site http://www.idrc.ca. CAB Publishing has recently launched a series of subject specific online communities catering to the needs of librarians and researchers, each community feature a comprehensive abstract databases with 25 years archive.

The library and information professionals can easily browse through the current publications available on various web sites in their area of interest, confirm the prices, etc. and place the orders online.

Any discrepancy in the invoices or bills, edition of books, printing, etc., can be clarified within minutes through e-mail and much of the paper work is reduced. It is expected that in near future, the Internet will become the mechanism for distribution of three fourth of the specialized journals and also the major medium for transfer of research information.

The librarians will thus need to change their attitude towards collection development, as the technology advances in future, it will encourage access to document rather than ownership. In future, virtual libraries may replace traditional libraries which means there would be purchase of access to information rather than the source.

(ii) Technical Processing : Preparing standard catalogue without much effort has become possible due to Internet and the world wide web. Librarians can check -the catalogues of other libraries like that of Library of Congress and confirm the information required for a record which can be easily ascertained from the original document. The library professionals can also access Internet resources for verification and downloading the bibliographical information from other institutions. OPACs via Internet have become a popular source of bibliographic information. Libraries can make use of other institutions by OPACs to get information they need to organize knowledge. Databases of bibliographic utilities will become more comprehensive source of information than has been so far possible by their present catalogues. With advance information retrieval facilities, the libraries in future will have added value by using catalogue of journal articles.

The librarians can provide the bibliographical data through Internet access via OPACs of other libraries in the world. The electronic documents can be supplied to the users on demand through the network. According to Schmidt, "access to OPACs will be increasing from outside the library. The boundaries between the cataloguing of libraries holding and cataloguing of information will be more difficult than today, in my opinion they will vanish completely when networks have reached a certain technical capacity."

Internet has also affected the traditional classification system of our libraries. Several libraries arc opting the Cyber Dewey Decimal Classification Summaries as a way to organize and navigate resources on the WWW. The Cyber Dewey website includes alphabetical index to Dewey. The Dewey home page (http://www.oclc.org/pp) division contains links to some of these systems. Joan Mitchell, the editor of DDC says, "it is exciting time to be Dewey user because we have a commitment to keep pace with knowledge to help our users to classify efficiently and help our users extend from the shelves of their libraries into the electronic environment."

(iii) Circulation : The Internet has made the circulation of in-house document much easier. After the technical processing, the new books documents can be placed in the OPAC on the day of acquisition itself and readers with Internet connection at home or at university can browse and reserve the books sitting right at their offices or at home, within seconds after arrival of the book in the library.

Further libraries subscribing to electronic journals need not necessarily provide access to it in the library. Since each subscription is provided, with a user ID, the reader by enquiring the user ID from the circulation section can access the journals from their departments or offices without taking pain of visiting the library.

Through Internet, the libraries can also provide bibliographical databases via OPACs from libraries of other institutions world wide. The OPACs may be searched from a terminal within the originating library or from a terminal located at a remote place.

(iv) Reference and Information Service : Internet for reference work in the library is gaining popularity. Reference librarians may use a multitude of information sources to answer the question they are asked, which are called ready reference collection. The Internet can be successfully utilized for providing short-range and long-range reference service because various primary and secondary sources of information are available online from many sites. Several sites like http:/kiz.at.ymas.edu.irre.html provides alphabetical listing of a full text resources data suitable for ready reference.

The URL http://www.refdesk.com, exposes the librarian to an excellent virtual library for reference source known as 'My Virtual Reference Desk'. Similarly India World http://www.india.com, is a comprehensive reference service on the net. The IFLA World Directory of National Union Catalogue is now available on IFLANET, at http://www.ifla.org/vl/2/due, this is a complete listing of all known current national union catalogues, including monographs, serials and general union catalogue and a hot link is also included for direct access for the catalogue which are available on the Internet.

(v) Communication : Internet has become the primary mode of communication which carries more than the combined total of the postal services of all countries in the world. It is an important means of communication which provides a cheap and efficient means of mail transfer. Libraries can use this facility extensively to communicate with the publishers, book sellers and vendors of the other library products and services with scholars librarians and users across the globe. The most popular means of communication on the Internet is e-mail. Like the regular mail, there are also mailing lists to user groups of people. These mailing lists often called *Listservs*, can serve a valuable resource for the librarians. A more public electronic forum for discussion on the Internet is called the Usenet News. Usenet provides large numbers of news groups or conference that have open participation which can be used by the library users and library professionals.

(vi) Resource Sharing and the Internet : Librarians can have access to the catalogue of various libraries attached to the universities and colleges in the world and accordingly place a request for their users. The increase in the cost of documents for many disciplines in recent years has meant that the libraries have been able to provide less and less access to research literature through their in-house collection. Also with the financial constraints, the librarians and information professionals are seeking alternative means of providing access to the journals. The problem of print journals and the concomitant development of computers and communication technologies have lead to the development of electronic alternatives to print journals, i.e., in various forms of electronic journals.

Recently, a number of publishers have agreed to offer their journals electronically to libraries through First Search Electronic Collection Online. This enables the libraries to subscribe a large collection of academic journals from many publishers from a single *www* interface that support cross journal searching and extensive browsing.

(vii) Inter-Library Loan (ILL) : The traditional inter-library loan operations are quite time consuming and labour intensive. With the advent of new technology, the electronic documents and various inter-library management tools such as software like Ariel and Avis have facilitated the libraries to share their resources effectively and efficiently.

Ariel software opens the window on Internet document transmission. The Ariel workstation developed by Research Libraries Group, lets users send and receive crisp clear copies of document over the Internet with speed and ease of fax. Avis is another Canadian product developed at the University of Waterloo and refined with the cooperation of inter-library loan practitioners in libraries across Canada and USA. It is PC based software designed to manage all aspect of inter-library loan process. The inter-library loan office can network multiple Avis workstation on local area network. It offers the following benefits:

(a) Single comprehensive solution for the management of all ILL activities.

(b) Effective management of the paper work and record keeping acquired in borrowing and lending an item.

(c) Status tracking of request at all stages of the ILL process.

(d) Integration of bibliographic and location information from CD-ROM catalogue and online union catalogue.

(e) Transparent electronic transmission of requests and messages through the Internet.

Thus with the help of these software, inter-library loan over the Internet has become of great assistance in the inter-library lending and borrowing. Retrieval has become easier and transaction much quicker as the request can be sent through e-mails.

Q. : What are the Flow-charts? Giving the types of Flow-charts, discuss their merits and demerits.

Ans. Flow-Charting, as a subject matter, comes under the purview of Systems Analysis and also associated with the decision on review of application software. In most applications, the software development process beings with a detailed study of the existing operations or combinations of operations, which accomplish the task or tasks to be computerized. This study is termed as a "Systems Analysis''. The main objectives of 'Systems Analysis' are two fold:

i. To improve the existing library system: and/or

ii. To replace the existing system with a new one.

During the last five years most of the system analysists have focused primarily on the improvement of manual operations in the libraries as well as previously automated applications. Whether its subject is manual or automated, a Systems Analyst determines what is being done in an existing library system; whether, and to what extent, it is deficient, and what alternatives for improvement exist.

The Systems Analyst uses data gathered by myriad methods to prepare a narrative description of the task performed within the library system (usually, in an automated library system) being studied. This narrative descripting, which may be embodied in a formal report or in an informal working document(s), is often supplemented by tabular or graphic presentations. Similarly, the movement of documents or information is usually depicted through the use of charts consisting of interconnected, labeled symbols, which represent various system components or work-steps. The flow chart is the most firmly established and widely encoured example of such graphic analytical tools

A flow chart is a schematic representation of the overall process that provides a clear and concise picture of the logic and flow of information in the programme of instructions. In other words, a flow chart represents a systematic way of carrying out a process, and is of immense use and helpful while writing a computer programme (say, in an automated / computerized library system) because, it represents the programmer with a *diagrammatic representation of the logic in* a given procedure. Thus, a flow chart is a pictorial description of time-sequenced activities and logic to be performed by computer for carrying out data processing on computer.

Types of Flow-charts

The flowcharts can be of four types –

- Sequential Flow Chart
- Branch/Jump Flow Chart
- Loop Flow Chart
- Nested Flow Chart

(1) Sequential Flow Chart

Sequential flow chart is considered as the most simplest and easiest kind of flow chart, involving no decisions, branches or loops (see Figure-1).

This flow chart is also termed by many as 'uni-directional' and/ or 'one-way traffic' flow chart.

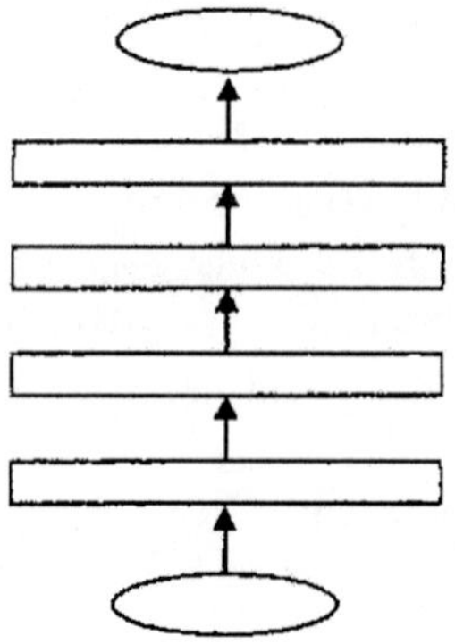

Fig. 1. Sequential Flowchart

(2) Branch/Jump Flow Chart

In this type of flowchart, usually one or more decision boxes are introduced and the action is taken depending on the result of the concerned decision element. Fig. 2 demonstrates a schematic representation of Branch flow chart.

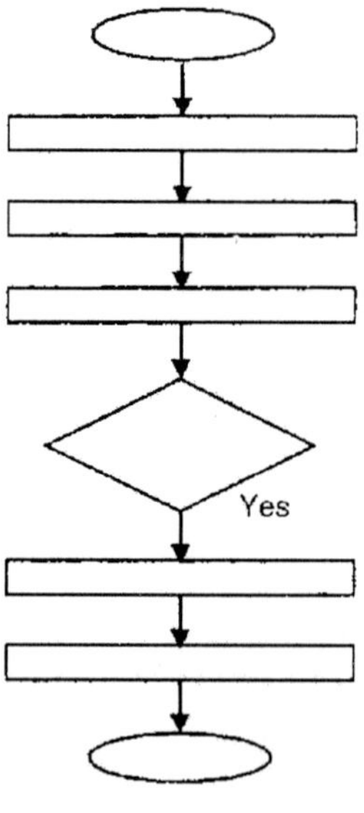

Fig. 2. Branch Flowchart

(3) Loop Flow Chart

This flow chart represents a procedure which may be repeated a definite number of times. Some term this flow chart as 'encircle-flowchart'. Each decision box in this flow chart could be used repeatedly depending upon the requirement and emerging changes and situations in a system. Fig. 3 depicts a schematic representation of Loop flow chart.

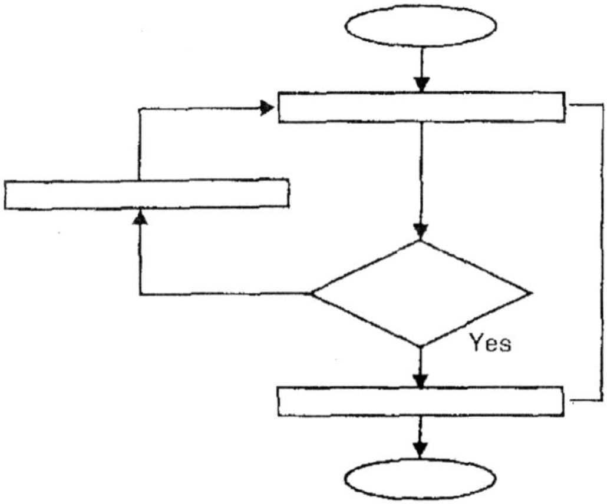

Fig. 3. Loop Flowchart

(4) Nested Loops Flow Chart

This flowchart denotes the involvement of several loops and branches. Thus, it is more complex and difficult to use, compared to the other three flow charts.

Levels of Flow Charts

A Flow chart can be prepared at several levels. These levels include:

- Block level
- System level
- Programme level

(i) Block Chart shows the sequence of main procedures within a system without showing in detail how they will be carried out. Blocks or rectangles define the different areas of activity, and flow lines connect them in the appropriate logical manner.

(ii) System Flow Chart on the other hand, expands each rectangle of block chart by breaking down each procedure into more details in order to describe the entire system. Such a cherty would be considerably longer than the block chart, and it is often necessary to divide it into sections with connector symbols used to denote the points where each section is connected to the next.

(iii) Programme Flow Chart defines in detail what operations the computer will perform, and using the chart, instructions will be encoded in a form suitable for the machine to accept. It becomes imperative on the part of the programmer to know what it to be done before starting to do it. Thus, it is exigent that the programmer knows the purpose and intent of a programmer before beginning to write that programme. The scientific planning for fully defining a specific solution to the point of implementation of computer is essential. Starting with a general view of the essential steps in a programme, details are added layer by layer until a detailed plan in the form of flow chart and/or several decision tables is/are produced.

Merits and Demerits of Flow-charts

Flow charts are extremely useful during programming analysis and offer several benefits to the system in general and the programming in particular. Some of these benefits that deserve mention are the following.

(i) **Helpful to enhance Understanding of Procedures:** Flowcharts help to enhance understanding of a current and proposed procedures, which ultimately help to grasp relationships quicker.

(ii) **Role in Problem Analysis and Synthesis :** The flow chart becomes a model of a programme/system that can be broken down into detailed parts for study. Synthesis provides combination of the various parts into a whole entity. Thus, flow charts may be used as effective working models in the design of new programmes and systems.

(iii) **Aids Effective Communication :** Flow charts provide valuable information, which cannot be expressed by thousand of words. It aids in communicating the facts of a problem to those whose skills are needed in the solution.

(iv) **Provide Effective Documentation :** Documentation is an important programming activity which include information like, need and purpose of programme; description of system; description of programme; listing of operator instructions; description of programme; controls; and maintenance.

Flow charts certainly render good and effective documentation. Good documentation is highly essential for organization so that it does not remain confined to original designer and subsequent modification will be easier and can be done with better understanding of part programme documentation which usually involves collecting, organizing, storing, and the otherwise maintaining a complete historical record of programmes and the other documents associated with the system.

(v) **Aids Effective Coding of Instructions :** Flow charts act as a guide during programme writing stage. Instructions coded in a programming language may be checked against the flow chart to ensure that no steps are omitted or ignored. Thus, they aid in effective coding of instructions.

(vi) **Useful during Debugging :** The term, 'debugging' denotes detection, location, and removal of mistakes in a computer programme. Some languages like, FORTRAN, BASIC etc., have built in a debugging programme within them. Thus, Flow charts play a crucial role in aiding in detection, location, and in removal of errors, if any, found in programming, there by ensuring the programme error free.

Inspite of its numerous advantages, flow charts are not free from pitfalls. The following pitfalls and limitations are usually experienced in a schematic representation of the over all process in the process of providing a clear and concise picture of the logic and flow of information in the programme of instructions.

(i) Though flow charts are quite easy to follow but their translation into computer programmes *is not easy* as it appears;

(ii) Complex and detailed flow charts are not only *labourious* to plan and draw, but also quite *cumbersome* and take a long time to *draw;*

(iii) Flow charts are supposed to be machine independent as well as free from computer language details. Very often details relating to the particular machine or language are introduced inadvertently at quite an early stage there by resulting in *loss of generality* of these flow charts; and

(iv) Action to be taken in specified situations can be difficult when many decision paths are involved.

Inspite of these limitations, the flowchart will continue to dominant as a coding guide for the programmer and in the process of analysis and solution of problems in a given computerized library system.

Q. : Write an essay on Software.

Or

Write short notes on –

– Operating system

– Application Software

– System Software

Or

What do you mean by Software? Listing the different types of Softwares, briefly discuss some of the operating systems.

Ans. A varieties of works in multifaceted form are carried out in a computer based on a given set of instructions. The sequence of instructions are written syntax in language which is known as Computer Programs. The program regulates the processing activity of a computer. Software is a set of computer programs, procedures and associated documentation for the effective operation of the computer system. Thus, the term software indicates a set of computer programs, procedures and associated documents such as flowcharts, manuals etc. In broad sense of the term, the software is nothing but a collection of programs which explores the capabilities of computer hardware machine.

Types of Software

The computer software are broadly grouped into two types, such as

(i) Application and (ii) System Software.

(i) Applications Software

The application software is also termed as application package which embodies a set of more than one programs to perform multi-operations in a specified or designated area. It enables the computer system to solve a specific data processing task. Further, the application software is categorized into two forms i.e., (a) User Application programs and (b) Pre-written Software Package.

(a) **User Application Programs :** Generally application programs are provided by the computer manufactures or suppliers but in many cases the user produces his own application programs. These programs are known as user application programs; for example a user may have payroll program or stock control program etc.

(b) **Pre-written software :** The pre-written software packages are ready to use programs, requiring no modifications. The packages developed meet all the broad and specific requirements of the users. The examples of such Pre-written Software Packages are:

- Word Processing/DTP
- DBMS
- Integrated Software Packages
- Text Retrieval Packages
- Software associated with Searching
- Library house keeping Softwares

(i) Word Processing/DTP

The application program that enable the processing of words is called the Word Processing Programs or Word Processor. A Word Processor is a software package that helps to create, manipulate the textual matter which is stored in files, edit the files, deletion of the text etc. Creating a document involves typing into the internal memory of the computer and saving it by writing it onto the disk. Editing the documents involves correction of the spelling mistakes if any, and deleting or inserting words, sentences or paragraphs. Libraries and information centers can use Word Processing Software in the preparation and updating of manuals, library guides and so on and in the generation of some forms, compilation of lists and in the production of catalogue cards. Word Processing Software should be able to permit the user to manipulate the text, as it is necessary in alignment of margins, in addition and deletion of paragraphs.

(ii) Data Base Management Software (DBMS)

It is a predetermined computer programming to control and

integrate a good quantum of data in a given file. Data Base Management Software package allows the user an interface more friendly with the computer system as compared to any high level language. Database Management Systems in general terms, have many attractions for the librarian willing to implement automation on a microcomputer. Due to its low cost, microcomputer becomes librarian's chosen instrument for developing computer applications. Also, software packages of varying power and capability are available for every known make of microcomputer.

There are three types of DBMS available to a microcomputer user. They are: (A) File (or data) management systems, (B) Relational DBMS, (C) Network and hierarchical DBMS. Of these, the first two types are easy to comprehend and do not call for intense knowledge in programming for developing library applications using them.

(A) File Management Systems: The main features of file management systems can be summarized as follows:

(i) they need no programming.

(ii) they are simple to set up and use.

(iii) they are menu-driven.

(iv) they are single file systems.

(v) they lack flexibility.

All that the librarian has got to do is to determine what is wanted from the file and devise an appropriate record structure. It is also important to devise a structure which facilitates data entry. The limitation of file management systems is that they can handle one file of data at a time.

(B) Relational Database Management Systems : These are called relational DBMS because the data that they can manipulate are stored as relations. The relations are in the form of data tables in which the information is arranged in rows and columns. The main features of relational DBMS may be summarized as follows:

(i) DBMS are command driven.

(ii) they are programmable to some extent.

(iii) they can work with more than one file at a time.

(iv) they need some degree of programming experience to gain the maximum benefit.

Instead of a limited number of choices from a 'menu', relational DBMS's provide the user with a command language in order to carry out the various operations. Secondly, a relational DBMS is able to access more than one file at a time, provided the files in question have at least one filed in common.

MS-ACCESS, FOXPRO, ORACLE are some of the examples of Data Base Management Software (DBMS).

(iii) Integrated Software Package

The business software integration has come into its own with the augmentation of Microsoft Office or MS-Office which is an Integrated Software Package to perform automation of every transaction of an office. LOTUS SMART SUITE or MS-office are an other example of Integrated Software Package.

(iv) Text-retrieval Packages

Text-retrieval is defined as the storage and subsequent retrieval of records from a computer system, the records being essentially textual rather than numerical, tabular or graphical. Although, each of the earlier mentioned software can be used for test retrieval purposes to certain extent, there are special purpose packages which have been written specially for the type of retrieval functions associated with libraries and information units. Some of the characteristic features of such software packages are: (a) the software is normally self-contained and can be set up with a minimum involvement of computer specialist staff; (b) the records in this software are independent, of variable length and are composed mostly of natural language texts; (c) access to data is by content rather than by structural position; (d) primary access is through inverted file of text terms drawn from the records as they are placed on the database. Thus, an important feature of such software packages is user interfaces, which allow a non-programmer to understand and use them directly without difficulty. Search and indexing facilities are the most important features of this type of software.

(v) Software Associated with Searching Online Retrieval Systems

Each of the major online systems has its own software which supports its activities on a host computer. Most of these hosts have begun to offer 'private file' facilities, with the aid of which users can exploit the sophisticated software developed by supporting large databases with many searchers. If the user is already familiar with the command language etc. of the host, then a private file on that system avoids the need for familiarization with a further software package. Private file facilities are expensive since a telecommunication charge is incurred every time a host computer is used. The second category of software generated in association with online searching of external databases, enables more economic access to the host systems. There are various packages which support online interaction with an external database and permit as for example, the development and editing of search profiles and search outputs locally.

(vi) Library House Keeping Software

There is a variety of packages, which are specially designed to support library house keeping routines such as acquisitions, cataloguing, circulation control and serials control. Some of these are integrated packages covering many functions; for example, Libsys; while others concentrate on specific functions including cataloguing, management information of various kinds as CDS/ISIS.

2. System Software

The system software is also known as systems package which is a set of one or more programs designed to control the operations of a computer system. System software does not contain any program which can solve specific problems but, general programs are written to assist human beings in the use of the computer system by performing tasks, such as controlling all of the operations required to move data into and out a computer and all the steps required in executing an application program. Thus, these are a collection of master programs which are specially designated to operate the system and control its activities. The system software supports the Application Software in following ways :

(i) Running the other Software.

(ii) Communicating with peripheral devices such as printers, disk and tape drives.

(iii) Development of other type of Software.

(iv) Monitoring the use of various hardware resources such as memory, peripherals, Central Processing Unit (CPU) etc.

The development of system software is called System Programming. The utility of system programming is to increase the productivity and efficiency of various applications for operating in a computer. System Programming is primarily achieved using assembly language or some middle level language like C which involves a technical knowledge as the programmer has to directly interact with the hardware of the computer.

The primary facet of the system software is the Operating System (OS) which regulates all the activities of the computer. MS-DOS, PC-DOS, OS/2 Wrap, VMS, MultiFinder, MVP, DOS/VS, UNIX, XENIX, Linus, Windows 95/95/2000, Windows NT etc. are some of the examples of the system software. Compilers of the various languages are also in the category of system software.

1. MS-DOS

Micro-soft Disk operating System or MS-DOS was developed by Microsoft for use on 16-bit PCs built around Intel's 8086 and 8088 chips in 1981.

Version 2 to 6.2 of this OS offers certain useful features like installable device drivers. These are routines used to control such devices as the keyboard and monitor, the disk devices and the printer. This makes it easier for the computer manufacturers to interface their hardware to this OS.

The current versions of this OS have incorporated many features found in the UNIX and XENIX operating system, such as file management, command mode, input-output redirect and the like. Inter process communications, using pipes allow the MS-DOS user to construct complex data processing tasks out of OS utilities. The enhanced versions of this OS run in the same manner on different computers and, also with these versions different applications can run together on the same computer, sharing common data files.

Well known variants of MS-DOS include IBM PC-DOS and APPLE-DOS.

MS-DOS basically works on three system files –

- IO.SYS
- MSDOS.SYS
- COMMAND.COM

MS-DOS is partitioned into layers to isolate the logic of the Operating System and the user-perception of the system from the hardware, it is running on.

The layers are divided into two types such as,

(i) Basic input/output System (BIOS)

(ii) Kernel

(i) Basic input/output System (BIOS) : The files or the contents which reside in the Read-only-Memory (ROM) chip is known as Basic input/output System (BIOS) and this contains programs to handle the primitive devices like keyboard, monitor, printer and system clock.

(ii) Kernel : It controls the hardware of the computer system and is being controlled through on and off at programs' command. For example, the Kernel directs the computer to read the names of the files from disk once a 'dir' command is given to the computer system. Kernel is a collection of hardware independent services called system functions. DOS Kernel is nothing but collection of two files. DOS Kernel is IO.SYS and MSDOS.SYS.

IO.SYS : It is the basic input/output software and acts like an interface between the core of the Operating System and the input/output capabilities of the computer. Keyboard, mouse etc., are input devices and printer, screen are the output devices.

MSDOS-SYS : This is DOS's main Kernel and acts like a file and disk manager.

Shell : Shell is the user interface of the operating system In MS-DOS the shell is nothing but the COMMAND.COM which processes and executes the user commands and the system functions accordingly. It may be noted here that the commands that the user make with the system are of two types and combination of these two types is known as Batch Command.

The three types of commands are:

a. Internal Commands

b. External Commands

c. Batch Commands

(a) Internal Commands : These commands are known as the Resident Commands which can be executed at any given point of time after booting without needing any other file except COMMAND.COM. All the internal commands are the memory resident commands and get executed from Random Access Memory (RAM).

(b) External Commands : These commands are also known as

Disk Based Commands which are actually executable programs given along with OS DOS and these reside in the hard disk or floppy disk. For executing these commands in the computer, respective executable files are required which are stored in primary memory of PC. When the command is over, the external command file gets removed from the memory of the system. For further execution of the same command, again loading of the commands of the same file is required.

(c) Batch Commands : Batch files are collection of commands, which may be internal or external commands.

2. UNIX

This OS was originally developed by Ken Thomson in 1970 for Bell Laboratories and was in the hands of researchers and universities for many years before its acceptance by the industry. UNIX OS is a layered system, with multi-user, multi-programming capabilities.

It is written in high level C language and is, therefore, less hardware dependent than OS written in lower level machine languages. This feature lends the characteristics of portability to UNIX, that is, it can be transported from one system to another.

The central piece of UNIX is referred to as the kernel. This is the master program that controls the computer's resources, allotting them to different users to do different task. The kernel, however, does not deal directly with the users. Instead, it starts up a separate interactive program for each user, called the shell, when the user logs on. The shell then acts as an interface between the user and the system, that is to say, the shall serves as a programming language, and as a command language interpreter. In its later role the shell reads the lines typed by the user and interprets them as requests to execute certain programmes. The competing demands of shells of different users are sorted out not by the shell but by the kernel, to decide exactly when each required program is to run. In the way the kernel and the shell cooperate for providing the UNIX service. The kernel keeps track of all the programmes being run, allotting time to each and decides when to stop and when to start another program. It also assigns space for files, runs the shell programs and handles the transfer of information between the computer and the input-output devices. In short, the kernel is the operating system. It communicates with the hardware. When something is types on the keyboard, the kernel collects the input and delivers it to the shell, for execution. The shell executes it and thereafter returns a prompt to the user for the next command. Supposing there is a command (or system call), requiring only a file to be copied, then the kernel finds space on the disk for the new file and keeps track of the relevant information such as the location, size, etc. of the file.

In UNIX each particular task is called a process. The commands or system calls are the basic routines. If a system call is used to open a file, then part of the kernel does so. Each part of the kernel accomplishes a specific basic task. Thus one system call may be for opening a file, the other may be for reading the file and yet another for closing the file.

The shell also has a few built-in commands, but most commands are separate programs stored within the computer. When a command is given (say, day) the shell searches for the file named day and if there is an executable program in the file, the shell starts execution of the program and after finishing the job goes into the waiting mode.

UNIX also has a library of programs written in C programming language. These program use system calls to handle interface between programs and the hardware.

An important feature of UNIX is what are called the shell scripts. These are the files that contain a list of other UNIX commands. When the shell script is run, the entire list of commands in the gets run.

In UNIX, every file is assigned to a directory, which can be viewed as a specialized form of file that maintains the list of all other files, that is to say, sub-directories of the original directory.

For file creation, the kernel allots space in the computer's memory storage, typically a disk. The text is stored one character per byte of memory. An anode entry is also created in a section of the disk to contain such information as the location of the file on the disk, the size of the file and when the file was last used/changed.

Also created is a directory entry, which by itself is a file. It contains the anode number of a file and the user-selected name for that file. Files themselves consist of a stream of bytes. The directory links the user-selected name for the file with the internal name, that is, the anode number.

Input-output devices are associated with special files in the directory. Programs use files and input-output devices interchangeably for input and output. The program first sees the stream of files flowing into it without bothering about the source and destination.

The UNIX system also provides the facility of pipes, which enable one program to be connected with another, after filtering it with the help of a program to be connected with another, after filtering it with the help of a program termed filtrex.

UNIX also treats devices as files. This enables source command to work equally well with files, terminals, tape drive and other input devices.

3. Windows

Windows operating systems are the GUI or Graphics-User Interface operating systems. These are accompanied with several utility programs, including Backup, Disk Cleanup and Disk Defragmenter. These utilities can be accessed from the Systems Tool menu.

A backup can be just one file that you have copied to a floppy disk, or it can be a compresses copy of the contents of your entire hard drive. If you only have a few important files it may not seem necessary to go to the trouble of backing up other data. However, if your hard drive fails, your Word preferences, E-mail settings, and your Internet settings will be lost-not to mention programs you may have previously installed and any Windows settings.

Although modern hard drives superbly engineered all your precious documents cannot be replaced if something goes wrong unless you have backed up your data.

Folders : Various types of files are generated while working on the computer. The basic idea of folders or directories to keep your work organized and easy to find similar to the way file folders are organized in a normal un-computerized office. Different applications generate different types of files that distinguished by their extension (i.e. a dot followed by three characters). For example Word saves files in doc extension, Excel saves files as .xls extension, Power Point files are saved as .ppt extension. Similarly audio files are saved as .wav or .mp3, video files are saved as .mpg or .dat and Pictures are saved as .jpg or .tif.

The Microsoft Window's Windows Explorer lists all the drives, files and folders on your PC.

To create a folder, following steps are done.

- Click the drive in Windows Explorer where you want to create the new folder.

- On the **File** menu, point to **New**, and then click Folder. The new folder appears with a temporary name.
- Type a name for the new folder, and then press ENTER. The name of the folder should suit its contents.

Note : If you want to create a new folder within a folder, click the folder and then follow steps two and three above.

You can build a virtual filing cabinet by grouping folders together inside other folders. For example, inside your "Music" folder you could store all the music folders for films for which you have the songs or for example "video" and "audio". The software should also be installed where you can find it easily. It makes sense to group together similar programs in one easily accessible place. You can customize the way you view files and folders by setting them to hide or highlight the information they contain.

The information that generated internally in an organization could be put inside a computer hard disk by typing it in appropriate software. If it is a letter or note or memo then Word may be used. If it is the salary details of employees then Excel may be used. If a database has to be maintained then Access may be used or if some presentations are to be made then PowerPoint may be used to prepare slides. Images that are to put inside the computer may be scanned using a Scanner and then edited by the Image Editors. Likewise Graphics programs may be used to prepare graphics.

Q. : Write short notes on the following :

- **Bar-coding**
- **Computer viruses**
- **Data**
- **E-mail**
- **Number System**
- **On Line and Offline Processing**
- **Search Engines**
- **Telecommunication**
- **World Wide Web (WWW)**

Ans.

1. BARCODING

Barcodes are the self contained messages with information encoded in a series of black bars of varying breadths and white spaces between every two of them. The bars and spaces represent a series of characters or digits. These are readable only by a scanner which sends messages to the computer that decodifies the number of the digits. The computer identifies such bars as '0's and '1's (Zeros and Ones) and white blanks as 'off's or 'on's. Therefore, a barcode is a series of 'o's and '1's representing characters of digits in such a form that can be identified by computers only.

295600 295601

Fig. Bar-code Labels

The bar-codes are read by bar code scanners. The light flashed from the barcode scanner on the barcode label undergoes reflection at the white lines and absorption on the dark bands. This reflected light is collected back and is converted into electric pulses by the photoelectric circuitry of the scanner. Further these pulses are converted into binary information by the interface circuitry of the scanner before they are fed to the computer, for further processing.

Application of Barcoding in libraries

The barcodes in the libraries can be used in following ways :

(i) In a library, barcoding is most frequently used in circulation system. As a first step for introduction of barcodes in circulation control system, it is necessary that the holdings (complete database), accession numbers and member identification numbers are converted in barcodes. The barcodes for documents can be generated in house in the form of peel-off labels, laminated and pasted on each document. Library membership cards, eight per sheet are printed cut and laminated with pouches.

Once these initial procedures are over, the operation can be instantaneous, as the circulation software is also available. The borrower needs to present his barcoded identity card and the bar coded books for issue. The circulation staff scans with the laser scanner across the barcode on the member card. Immediately, the details of the user are displayed on the monitor and the cursor will stand at the accession number. Next, the barcode on the document is scanned. As in the case of member, the details of the documents are also displayed. The document can then be issued to the user. Multiple borrowing facility and computation of due date etc. are taken care of by the software.

(ii) Besides, with the help of a data gathering device, the barcodes can be used to verify stock, as libraries have to resort to stock verification, at intervals. If the provision for multiple barcodes or multi-dinesional barcoding is incorporated to handle call number information also, wrong shelving of books can be auto-detected which would help the staff to rectify the same. The individual journal volumes are handled in a library with lots of intricacies. Many a time, these issues have to be taken out of the display area for xerox work. There are also chances of their shelving in wrong cabinets. These problems are tackled a by using a control number for the current journal issues and barcoding them accordingly. A database of journal issues can thus be generated so that their management through cards can be avoided. If the parent institution also has a computerised accounting systems, all the bills can be routed after barcoding, using transaction or any other inventory number as the key field so that their follow up and processing are done efficiently.

2. COMPUTER VIRUSES

The Viruses are nothing but are the program which appear at a fix time and disturb the normal functioning of the computer. A virus just copies itself and spreads. A virus cannot move by itself, it must attach itself to another program. Viruses may be written to multiply, to damage other programs or to alter data. Viruses come in a wide variety; they are often small and well hidden, therefore difficult to find. They may be benign and result only in amusement or more annoyance, or they can be malignant and malicious. The various categories of viruses are:

- **Boot Sectors Infection :** Hides in the boot sector of a disk or the partition table of a hard disk and takes control of the computer system when it is booted. It then copies itself into the computer's memory. When other disks are used, the virus transfers to their boot sectors. The most common boot sector viruses are the

Pakistani Brain virus and the Stoned / Marijuana virus.

- **Application Program Infection :** The most infectious type of computer viruses is the application program infector or file virus. They may attach to any executable file usually to .COM and .EXE files. An application program infector takes control after the initial use of the infected program. Once the virus is in place in the RAM of the computer system, it will potentially infect every program run on the computer until the computer is shut off. The most widespread virus today is the Jerusalem virus.
- **Stealth Viruses :** These are the Viruses which attempt to hide their presence. Some of the simple techniques include hiding the change in date and time and hiding the increase in file size. Some even prevent anti-virus software from reading the part of the file where the virus is located. Some also encrypt the virus code using variable encryption techniques.
- **Dark Avenger Mutation Engine :** Polymorph encryption program used by virus developers to encrypt the virus in order to avoid detection. The engine uses a special algorithm to generate a completely variable decryption routine each time. No three bytes remain constant from one sample to the next.
- **Multipartite Virus :** This Virus infects both the boot sector of a disk as well as application programs.
- **Macro Viruses :** It is the Virus that attaches to a word-processing or spreadsheet file (typically an Ms Word of Excel file) as a macro. Once the file is accessed, it replaces one of the Word or Excel standard macros with an infected version, which can then infect all subsequent documents.

Viruses are usually passed via disk. You buy or are given a disk that already has the virus on it. Some PC viruses are only passed if you boot (start your computer) from an infected disk-turning your computer on with the disk already in the floppy drive. Otners can infect your system when you copy a file from an infected disk or even when you attempt to erase an infected disk. Viruses can also be passed when you use a modem to download a file from the Internet or access data or programs on a network. Before you get too paranoid about viruses, realize that most computer users have actually encounter one. The chances of contracting a virus are particularly small if you only install shrink wrapped available, shrink-wrapped programs and rarely exchange disks with anyone else. The more computers your system comes in contact with-via modem or via floppy disks-higher the risk.

A computer generally affects a computer by –

- Corrupting Data.
- Increasing File sizes.
- Interference with the display on the VDU.
- Formatting the hard disk, thus destroying data.
- Destroying the FAT (File Allocation Table, where DOS keeps information on each and every file stored on the disk).
- Marking good sectors bad.
- Destroying contents of sectors at random.
- Slowing down the system.
- Destroying the FAT or scrambling file names by manipulating the directory contents, the data is all there, but the user is unable to access it.
- Renaming all files with a single name.

The level of destructiveness of viruses varies widely. Some viruses display pictures or messages on the screen periodically. Others erase or destroy programs and data. They also wreak havoc at different speeds. Some viruses spread through your system fairly quickly but don't actually do anything for days or even months.

How does a Virus Work?

The first step of a virus is to initialize the computer. It remains hidden and tries to gain control from the operating system. The next step is for the virus to set up virus processing and modifies the system to support virus control. Then the virus wants to find available hosts. Its job is to seek new receptive hosts and determine if they are available for infection. They want to infect as many systems as possible. They infect the system by attaching themselves to the host. They moderate their infection activities to reduce the risk of being found. This is when a virus officially begins its destruction of a system.

A virus wants to determine its time to activate, which depends on a number of things. It needs to know the preset number of infections, the elapse time in the system, the preset data or time and other external events that have occurred. Depending on these factors the virus determines if it should be destructive at this time or if it should wait. At the end the computer is usually unaware of the infection.

Basically all a virus does is live in a host program. Each time the host program is executed, so is the virus. When the virus is executed, it seeks at least one other program to which it can copy itself. This is why a virus is constantly spreading.

Safe Computing

The spread of computer virus infections can be stopped through the practice of "safe computing." The following are a list of do's and don'ts for safe computing.

1. Do not use illegal software! If the software has been obtained illegally, how can you assume that it doesn't contain a virus.
2. Never boot your computer system from a diskette other than the original DOS diskette. Only one write-protected boot disk should be assigned to a floppy-based system. The diskette should be clearly marked, write-protected and used only for booting up the designated computer. If you accidentally try to boot from a non-system disk, turn the computer off and boot with the write-protected system disk.
3. If your system uses a fixed disk, never boot from a diskette. In some situations, write protection software for the hard disk should be employed.
4. Always write-protect your systems and program disks. Write-protect labs are easy to use and very effective. You should write only on data disks.
5. Only copy files from the original distribution disks.
6. Always keep at least one set of back-up copies of all original disks. This won't prevent a virus infection, but it will help in the recovery process if an infection occurs.
7. Do not loan out program disks. They may be infected when they are returned. If you must loan a disk, always check it for viruses or format it before using the disk on your computer system.
8. Never use a computer that has already been turned on by another user. Always use a cold boot to restart the computer. Do not assume that a warm boot will remove a virus.
9. Make all the .COM and .EXE system and program files read

only by using the command ATTRIB+R. Some viruses can now circumvent this method.

10. Always keeps a lookout for strange occurrences:
    - When you do a directory listing, look at the volume label;
    - Observe whether your computer system is slowing down;
    - Watch for files that disappear;
    - Notice when there are attempts to access the disks when there should not be any read or writes activity;
    - Watch whether the loading of programs takes longer;
    - Keep a lookout for decreases in the main memory or reduction of disk space;
    - Watch for unusually large sizes on program files;
    - Watch for recent creation dates on old program files;
    - Watch for unusual displays on the computer screen.
11. Use caution when using public domain and shareware software or any new software. There have been instances where commercial software has been sold with a virus.
12. If you are downloading software from a bulletin board or other computer network including the Internet, always download to a diskette. You should then scan the diskette for possible virus infections.
13. In a lab environment, do not allow users to run their own programs or boot the computer system with their own disks. Users should only have data disks that are not bootable. All program disks and hard disks in a lab must be checked frequently for viruses. If users are allowed to use their own program disks, they must be scanned before they are used in the computer lab.
14. Most important of all is to teach computer users about computer viruses so that they can recognize them. Computer users need to be able to identify viruses so that they are able to prevent their spread.

3. DATA

Data are the raw material and information is what we get after processing the data. To be more precise, data are raw facts and figures and information is processed data which is useful and meaningful data. Data are the input to processing and information is output.

How are data converted into information is explained in the figure:

Input				Processing	Output
Data				Total	
Roll No.	M1	M2	M3	(M1+M2+M3)	Roll No. 1 has scored maximum marks.
1.	40	52	68	160	
2.	48	38	67	153	
3.	74	39	45	158	

Data--Marks obtained by three students in three subjects respectively

Software calculates the total of marks for the students

Who has scored max marks is information for the class teacher

Data is a plural form. Singular form of data is "*datum*" which is rarely used.

Information distinguishes itself from data as it is more useful and meaningful. The marks of the subjects, as such are of no use for the teacher but then calculating the total helps him in finding out the ranks of the students. One information can be used as the data for taking out another information, e.g., total marks calculated above will serve as data to find out percentage and hence division of the students, to check how many students have scored distinction, first class, second class or failed. Information can be distinguished form data by some characteristics like *relevance, timeliness, accuracy, concise* and *complete*. Data should be accurate but may not necessarily possess rest of the characteristics. The characteristics of information are explained as:

(i) **Relevant :** The information should apply to the situation or the query or problem.

(ii) **Timely :** Information should be presented as and when required. For example, there is no point receiving newspaper after two-three days.

(iii) **Accurate :** Input and output should be accurate, so that no wrong decisions take place. A small mistake can lead to hazardous results.

(iv) **Reliable :** It should be reliable, i.e., there should not be any doubt about the presented information.

(v) **Concise :** It should not be unnecessarily lengthy, i.e., precision is an important characteristic of information.

(vi) **Complete :** All the important elements should be covered and nothing should be missed.

4. E-MAIL

E-mail is an electronic system which is an effective source of sending mesage from one place to another. Earlier, to send a message from one place to another was a time consuming factor. Today the information can be transmitted from one part of the world to another in a minute with the help of network of E-Mail.

In the process of E-mail, computer is clicked for windos-98 or other available OS and there are two options:-

1. Internet Explorer select (for Internet)
2. Outlook Express (for E-mail)

Having after selected second option, few more options appear on the screen and either new mail or compose is selected. Thereafter there is a space for self e-mail code and also the code to be sent for. Then related subject of the letter is noted and also the entire information is noted.

After this process E-mail information can be sent directly by a click or can be stored in out-box, if it is in out-box again 'send' is given as command and the information reaches immediately.

This complete process can be explained as given on next page :-

Windows-98

↓

- Internet Explorer: Select (Internet contact)
- Outlook Express (Through this you will be connected internet)

New mail Or compose	Reply	Reply All	Print	Del	Send	Func-tion

Select New Mail

From : Your E-Mail address

To : Address to send E-Mail

C.C. : Mean Carbon copy

Subject : As per your choice

Matter : As per your choice

This massage will be placed in out box or directly send. If placed in out box, click in the send.

The credit goes to computer for this all contribution. The need of the libraries of any part of the world of U.S.A., England or India, information can be sent with the help of Internet or E-mail within very few minutes while it was no so early to this period.

5. NUMBER SYSTEMS

Numbers have a vital role in human life. Human life and in its day to day activities can not be performed without numbers. The importance of number in human life is likewise the same importance is in computer operation and use. Computer is an electronic machine. It uses binary numbers. Here By-means two numbers. Therefore binary is that which uses two figures and numbers. These numbers are 0 and 1 which are quite essential since the computer is invented. The reason is that computer is operated by electronic and understands the language of 0 and 1. BIT word is short form of Binary digit. It is made of early two words BI and Digit word (Last) 1. BIT means two and eight number digit is made one BITE.

In order to understand basic facts of binary notation, decimal, octal number and hexadecimal should be clearly known.

(1) Decimal Number System : Decimal number system is used to do for every day works. Ten means 10 and ten numbers are as follows:-

0, 1, 2, 3, 4, 5, 6, 7, 8, 9.

The most important factor in decimal system is that highest number in this system is 9 and smallest number is 1. In the system the set of number is meant in 10 power. In a given number how much power of ten is, it is decided according to place of the number. To count the place value forward from right to left. Decimal notation system can be explained with the following example :

5461

	10^3		10^2		10^1		10^0
	5		5		6		1
	5 × 1000		4 × 100		6 × 10		1 × Nil
	5000		400		60		1
or	5000	+	400	+	60	+	1 = 5461

Any decimal number can be converted into Binary number. To convert decimal number into Binary, it is to be divided by 2 and remaining – is written at left respectively. This process continues till the result remains 0 Zero.

(2) Binary Number System : Computer works in a system in which there are two numbers only which are 0 and 1. The number of this system is called as Binary number or Bit. The value of a Bit may be 0 or 1. The base of Binary system is two therefore its place value becomes double from right to left respectively or say 1,2,4,8,16,32,64. etc. These numbers can be denoted in the power of 2 also which can be written as follows:-

2^0, 2^1, 2^2, 2^3, 2^4, 2^5, 2^6 etc.

The value of binary notation can be ascertained as follows:-

11101.

2^4	2^3	2^2	2^1	2^0
1	1	1	0	1
1×2×2×2×2	1×2×2×2	1×2×2	0×1	1×Nil

1×16	1×8	1×4	0	1
16 +	8 +	4 +	0 +	1 = 29

The advantage of binary system are as follows:

1. The base of this number might be any, but by this numbering all works can be possible which is not in others.
2. Computer is made of electronic components which work on the basis of on and off system.
3. The number collected in Binary systems can be recorded in an easy way into Magnetic tape, disc etc.
4. Electronic circuit can be made easily.

(3) Octal Number System : Its base is 8, therefore in this system the number 0 to 7 included. In many micro-computers, this system is used directly in input and output. The size of this system is in 8 and therefore the place value of maximum number from right to left comes 8 times. For example:

1, 8, 64, 512 etc.

Octal number system can be explained as per following example:-

5461

8^3	8^2	8^1	8^0
5	4	6	1
$5\times8\times8\times8$	$4\times8\times8$	6×8	$1\times$Nil
2560	256	48	1
	= 2560 + 256 + 48 + 1 =		3135

(4) Hexadecimal Number System : At present mostly computer making companies use the Hexadecimal number system and most computer gives the information in this system. The system includes the following numbering digits :

0, 1, 2, 3, 4, 5, 6, 7, 8 ,9, A, B, C, D, C, E, F etc.

6. ONLINE AND OFFLINE PROCESSING

Computer processing is the method in which input data are processed. There are various methods or techniques used for computer processing. Three standard methods of using computers are commonly found in information processing and in other areas of computer usage. They are : batch processing, online processing and real time processing.

(i) Batch Processing : This was one of the earliest methods of using computers developed during the period 1950s. Duding that period the dominant memory storage medium was magnetic tape. At that time magnetic tape offered relatively inexpensive bulk storage. Therefore batch processing was used for jobs that involved several thousands of routine operations such as were found in wages and salary preparations, stock controls and ledger maintenance aspects, etc.

The great disadvantage of the batch processing is the inability of the system to respond to individual enquiries – where a random enquiry may want to examine the individual record. Although, batch processing is an efficient method for routine large scale operations, it is rather inefficient and inflexible, where individual transactions are required at different times during the day and the response time is certainly more. Systems which utilized batch processing were known as offline systems and the information services rendered through such systems were termed offline service. In other words, the user of an offline information service could not directly interact with the system. For a long time SDI service was provided through batch mode only.

(ii) Online Processing : The development of magnetic disc memories offered rapid, random access to files of records and could be utilized as backing store. This development resulted in the emergence of many online processing systems. This form of processing allows random enquiries to be made to any concerning individual records and enables almost instant response to the queries. Fundamental to online processing is the provision of number of terminals connected to the processor. These terminals are usually either a key board and VDU combination or a telephone typewriter, which is a combination of typewriter and printer. Terminals, connected to the processor locally by cable or remotely by telephone line, allow different departments to have direct access to files held by the central processor. Databases can now be interrogated locally or remotely by different kinds of users.

In online processing the terminals allow users to access individual records and update their contents if necessary. Online processing is now widely used in several areas including information retrieval and document retrieval systems. The services rendered through online systems are known as online services. Many commercial companies are providing online bibliographic searches on payment basis. Some of these are : BRS/SEARCH, DIALOG, ORBIT, etc. These companies offer online information retrieval from many commercially available databases like CA SEARCH, INSPEC, COMPENDEX LEXIX, etc. Even in India, there is a commercial organization called Informatics India Ltd., Bangalore which provides to the end users online search services on payment basis. SDI services from databases like CA SEARCH, INSPEC, COMPENDEX, etc. were provided for some years by INSDOC in batch mode. Also, the Indian Institute of Science, Bangalore, under UGCs grant scheme operated searches from databases like CA search and INSPEC on an experimental basis. Of course, these services were made available to academic community. NISSAT (National Information System for Science and Technology), operating under the DSIR, has opened some regional search centers, which will serve the user community to provide online searches accessing some international databases using modems through commercial Networks like Telenet, etc.

(iii) Real-time Processing : Real-time processing is a special version of online processing. It has to deal with a rapidly changing environment where information must be as up-to-date as possible. The data is inputted and outputted at very high speeds to and from terminals, which are remotely located from the processor. Owing to the remoteness of the terminals great use is made in real-time processing of various telecommunications facilities to transmit and receive data. Real-time processing is used in many airline ticket reservation systems, banking transactions etc.

The SDI system actually started as a batch mode service in the initial stages of its existence. But, in the present day context, SDI services are also provided in online interactive mode depending upon the demand and facilities available in individual organizations. This has been made possible by advance made in computer and communications technologies.

(7) SEARCH ENGINES

Search engines are mechanisms which aid users to search the entire Internet for relevant, information. They are based on allowing users to enter keywords that are matched against a database. Unlike subject directories, which use human indexers to build their indexes, search engines use software programs which create automatically their own databases containing lists of web pages. Search engines are composed of three different parts: (i) a program called a spider (or robot or crawler), (ii) a database with an index and (iii) search software. Spiders wander through the web, crawling from site to site, following links between pages. Different search engines use different types of spiders, where as some visit every possible site, others are based on more selective principles and visit only the most popular sites. The first type of spider finds a huge volume of information in a short space of time, the second type generates a smaller number of pages with perhaps more relevant information. Every page found by a spider is stored in a database and an index of its contents is built by extracting automatically words from the web pages and ranking them alphabetically using some principles which inverted files use. The index is therefore, a list of every word, except stop words, with a pointer to its location on the database.

Again, different search engines will follow different principles. For example some will index every single word on every web page, while other search engines index only the title and top level phrases of a web site. The third element of the search engine is the search software, which is a program, which compares search queries keyed in by the users with the index, finds matches and ranks them in order of relevance. The criteria for judging relevance will vary according to the search engine.

Some of the popular Search Engines are :

* **ASKJEEVES** : (*http://www.aj.com*) - Jeeves is bright, friendly and works fast to answer your questions. This suggests more than one place to look for your answer, but doesn't overload you with useless sites that aren't relevant. The service – part human, part machine – is an effective mix.
* **ALTAVISTA** : (*http://www.altavista.com*) - This search engine is well established and huge. You get more search results back from Alta Vista than most other search engines. You can also ask other questions in plain English now. When you need to conduct a comprehensive search, Alta Vista should always be among your choice of search engines.
* **HOTBOT** : (*http://www.hotbot.com*) - A firm favourite with many veteran Internet users. HotBot gives good results and has designed its Web site so that it is simple and easy-to-use. If you are unsure about this search engine business, follow the step-by-step guide to search engines with HotBot on Internet

Advisor's Web site *www.netadvisor.co.uk.*

* **LOOKSMART :** (*http://www.looksmart.com*) - A fairly recent addition to the search engine fold Look Smart has become one of favorite search sites. It has created a particularly effective directory of sites, which logically categorizes all types of site and makes it easy progress to the Web site you want.
* **REDIFF :** (*http://www.rediff.com*) - Rediff has created a famous brand unique to the Indian Net scenario. It's one of the first places that new Indian sites submit to and it can give you results that other search sites don't. it is a clever all-rounder.
* **LYCOS :** (*http://www.lycos.com*) - Lycos has done a good job extending its brand and function by building search engines that search specifically for say MP3 or pictures. It has also recently launched a TV advertising campaign, which raised its profile.

  Other popular search engines are Yahoo and Google.

8. TELECOMMUNICATION

Telecommunication means new medias of fast communications of information system. These fast and high mediums developed suddenly which gave rise the need of computer application of libraries. These developments provides rights to the reader to get information on computer's sitting. Any communication media is operated by electrically or electromagnetically operated which includes Radio, Television, Telegraph, Telephone. Telephone connecting with computer and modem gave birth to networking and thus the use increased.

It resulted to the fast development of communication systems and the computer based library services are developed. Some media of communication systems are as follows:-

(1) Telecommunication Satellite : Satellite communication is new and effective media of information system. With the help of satellite, the changes and wave communication in space can be noted and caught at the earth. Presently, India and other countries of the world are using satellite in information collection.

(2) Telex : Telex is that technology of telecommunication which helps text and graphic information on the television screen. The user can select talent pages with the help of decoder and Key pad. The picture of television is made by vertical lining system. It was developed by BBC Engineer and other officers in the year 1920 according to British standards – word system. Telex was made on the pattern of European standards.

(3) Teleprinter : Teleprinter is an effective media of communication. Any document can be printed with the help of computer. Since teleprinter technology developed, it made easy the telecommunication.

(4) Teletext : The system was developed in the year 1972 by B.B.C. It is one way system of communication and can be received the readable material on the computer. This technique is based on the telephone. The information is received on telephone and in the similar way teletext provides speedy information on telecast.

(5) Videotext : For information collection and display, Videotext is a new technique. Transmitting text and graphic is stored in computer database. It is used for renewal of encyclopedias, dictionary treatise publications. It is used for SDI and documentation services too.

(6) Tele Conference : This conference is based on telephone and computer, means the subjects and topics to be discussed in conference can be heard on telephone and seen on T.V. screen. Thus the proceedings and happenings in conferences and seminars at national or international levels can be interviewed at its own place or wherever needed.

(7) Voice in the Free Network : One of the newer technologies that have spring from the need to transmit voice over data networks is Voice over Internet Protocol (VOIP). Generally, it is referred to as Internet telephony. It enables voice to be carried over IP – based, packet-switched networks. So far the voice network could only later to voice and not data communications. This obviously meant every thing to be duplicated; line rental, servicing, and installation, call cost and inconvenience. This situation still exists today despite data networks such as the Internet or a private company network having plenty of unused available space or bandwidth.

(8) E-learning : Every vendor trying to sell his e-learning solution and has his every own definition of the term. It could be learning off the web, putting up lessons on the corporate Internet, video broadcasting, CD-ROM based training in conjunction with real time on line personal help or a combination of these elements. One can learn almost anything with e-learning, from computer basics to programming, technologies and soft skills like management and plenty more. The advantages of e-learning are many. One could have employees anywhere in the world and still make the same training content available to them. One also save time on traveling to attend training sessions. The contents can also be made available quickly to that training and can happen in time for your projects to start. Learning need not happen only when the classroom sessions get scheduled. E-learning also gives room for each persons learning style and pace, leading to better retention and comprehension.

(a) **Biometrics :** Biometrics relies on distinctive individual physiological traits; within such traits, on a (Deoxyribo Nuclear Acid) - the hereditary materials that determines what genetic traits we inherit – is supposed to be the most distinctive. It is like a code that directs our body cells to make or assemble things that are required for the functioning of our body. Though within such a large molecule, a first glance will not show up a significant difference in the code even a single insignificant changes in the sequence leads to the differences that we see.

DNA matching has advantages over other means of biometric verification. The human ability to look at a face, memorize it and recall it when you meet the same person again is entering the domain of the computer called facial recognition. This technique enables the computer to use your face as your password or identify criminals by looking at photographs of a crowd and matching these to an existing database.

Face recognition can be used widely – from authenticating people for access to computer networks bank ATMs etc., through smart cards to searching for terrorists on criminals in crowded places for surveillance or on voter's ID cards or passports to prevent fraud. Taking this to the extreme, however, may soon lead to a day when big brother is watching you become an every day reality.

Thus, computer has made easy the communication systems and resources with more speedy and effective since before.

9. WORLD WIDE WEB (WWW)

The WWW is the multimedia part of the Internet displaying a hyper text type of structure and search facilities. It was first developed for sharing documents between the nuclear physicists of the European Particle Physics Laboratory (CERN) in Switzerland in 1989, by Time Berners, a British Engineer. His idea was the text of each document could contain references (or links) to other documents, and these links would be 'live'. That is, the reader could make an immediate move directly to the document being referred to, or even to a specific place in it. It was not a wholly new concept – hypertext, as it was called, but was already available for use on some desktop computers. The new element was the idea of linking to documents on other computers on different networks. The ability of the hypertext to take the reader directly from document to document made a perfect marriage with the Internet's ability to interconnect computers all over the world at minimal cost. Something new was born; the *Word Wide Web* – "the web' for short.

The main characteristics of the WWW organization and structure are :

(i) Organize documents into pieces of information (pages) using a set of rules which tag and format the documents, the Hypertext Mark up Language (HTML).

(ii) Every individual document or page is assigned a unique address, called the Uniform Resource Locator (URL).

(iii) Each URL can be linked with a hypertext type line to other URLs and even pieces of information within each document (buttons) can be linked to URLs to other pieces of information.

(iv) These documents can be searched through interactive interface programs which allow users to browse and navigate through the documents and are called Web browsers.

(v) The communication between the Web browsers and the Web servers is regulated by a common language using a standardized set of rules called Hypertext Transfer Protocol (HTTP). The HTTP allows the interpretation of the HTML signs within each Web page in order to display correctly the page and to enable the transfer of files. A client programme or Web browser provides the user with control over the retrieval process and also over the links to be activated.

It is to be noted that individuals and organizations create home pages to present their own information or services. A collection of home pages located on the same server is called a Web site. Access to these pages is via the uniform Resource Locator (URL) using a browser. Some examples of browsers are Lynx, Netscape, etc. These addresses link the user to the host computer and their individual files, these are then displayed on the user's terminal or workstation. With the help of appropriate software users can read documents, view pictures, listen to sound, and retrieve the information.